10 STEPS TO

SALES SUCCESS

Other books by Simon

Messages from your Self

Unlock the hidden secrets
of your Birth Code

Leap into Love

Learn the secret to passionate
and LASTING relationships

How to Raise
a Happy Child

... and make your Self happy too!

10 Steps to
Break Through Fear

A little book that packs
a very BIG PUNCH

Lessons from Tyson

The story of a rescue dog
who rescued me right back

(More information on how to order at the back of the book)

10 STEPS TO
SALES SUCCESS

Double your income...
and TRIPLE your fun!

By Simon H Firth

Simon Firth
 EMINARS

Published by Simon Firth Seminars
Sydney, Australia

Published by Simon Firth Seminars, Sydney, Australia

Printed by CreateSpace, Charleston, USA

Distributed by CreateSpace and Simon Firth Seminars

Cover design: Bear Essentials, Sans Souci, Sydney
Cover photos: iStock/Getty

ISBN-13: 978-1497562172
ISBN-10: 1497562171

Edition: 1.1

About the author

SIMON H Firth is a professional writer, presenter and personal growth expert who specialises in teaching success strategies and advanced communication skills.

He is the founder of Simon Firth Seminars and the author of six books about finding your happiness: with your children, your partner and, above all, with your Self.

Simon has worked as an editor, a writer, a salesman and a sales trainer in England, Canada and Australia.

He was the No.1 sales executive in Australia for peak-performance experts such as Anthony Robbins, Tom Hopkins, Jim Rohn and Wayne Dyer.

Simon is also a devoted animal lover and donates 10 per cent of all his earnings to the Worldwide Fund for Nature (formerly World Wildlife Fund).

He lives and teaches in Sydney, Australia.

Acknowledgements

I AM deeply indebted to my business mentor and teacher Anthony Robbins, who introduced me to the powerful science of neuro-linguistic programming (NLP) when I worked for his organisation in Vancouver, Canada, many years ago.

I believe that Tony is still far and away the No. 1 sales trainer and peak performance coach in the world, and I urge those of you who have not already done so to read his books and, if you can, attend his live events. They are simply life-changing.

I have included in this short book many of the key NLP techniques I learnt from Tony, which I have since refined over many years of using them in the field. I have also included a wealth of material that I developed in my time as a salesman and sales trainer in Australia, Canada and the UK. Plus, I have added a tonne of information gleaned from reading more than 200 books and attending countless seminars on the subjects of personal development and human potential over the past 35 years.

I am profoundly grateful to every one of my teachers. I owe everything I am and everything I do to each and every one of you.

Contents

- - -

Introduction:
The best job in the world

I WANT to congratulate you on finding your way to this material. It means you are ready to take the next step in sales... and in life.

I also want to say right up front that this is not a conventional sales training course in any way. There are many excellent sales courses around, and most of them contain some very good advice on how best to frame your sales pitch. The trouble is that all of us in life have become almost immune to being sold because these days it happens to us everywhere we go – on the TV, at the movies, on the phone, and every time we go online.

Even at petrol stations the attendants are always trying to upsell us to buy chips or flashlights or three Mars bars for the price of two.

And this is especially true in business, isn't it?

Most of the people you will be talking to – managers, marketing directors, business owners, even householders and consumers – already know all the standard sales patter almost as well as you do.

So you need to be different. You need to stand out. And that means you need to learn some new sales and customer relations skills that the others aren't using so that when your customers meet you and hear your pitch, they feel it is new and refreshing – and above all they feel that it is ENJOYABLE for them.

* * *

The main focus of this course is to teach you how to master the art of communication so that you will be able to speak directly to a person's subconscious mind, where true influence takes place.

You will become expert at a whole range of advanced subliminal techniques that hypnotists and therapists use every day to bypass a person's fears.

You will also learn how to empower yourself to perform at your peak, making you much more effective than you may have been in the past in influencing others to buy your product or service.

The reason I say this with such confidence is that these techniques work. I have used them myself with great success, and I know many others who have as well.

What this means for you is that you will be able to

connect with your customers on a much deeper level, quickly and easily.

And what this REALLY means for you is you will be able to make more sales and more money in the next few months and years than you ever dreamed possible – AND have ridiculous amounts of fun in the process!

* * *

So why is this book different?

What sets this material apart from the others is that it puts the emphasis not just on what you do or say when you are in front of a client, but on how you FEEL.

Specifically, I want you to realise that the happier you are and the more fun you have, the more sales you will make and the more money you will earn.

Look around you. There's not enough focus on having fun these days, is there? Especially in business, and especially in sales. It all gets so serious. "Make your budget... or else!"

Now tell me if you disagree, but I would argue that we are at our most effective – and therefore our most powerful when it comes to influencing others – when we are having fun and enjoying ourselves.

We are therefore likely to make significantly more money when we are happy.

Why? Simply because the most important lesson you will ever learn as a sales professional is that your goal is to be so infectiously happy and upbeat that your positive energy rubs off on your customers, leading them to buy both you AND what you are offering them.

* * *

Selling is a transfer of energy

I would go even further and say the ability to be happy – to feel good – is the most important quality you can ever cultivate, not just in sales but in your life.

<u>Write this on a card and keep it with you:</u>
Sales success starts with FEELING GOOD.

Think about this. When you are feeling good the world is beautiful. Customers are beautiful. Even your grumpy boss is no longer such a pain in the arse. In fact, instead of resenting negative and angry people, you can now start to feel sorry for them that they are missing out on all the juice of life.

Above all, when you are feeling good you are going to be more effective in influencing others.

And that's all sales is, isn't it? The art of selling is the art of influencing someone to buy YOU first, and then your product or service second.

Selling is all about the transfer of energy. And when you are feeling good you are able to transfer that vibrant, positive energy to your customer.

As humans we are all giving and taking energy all the time, aren't we? The next time you have coffee or lunch with someone, notice where your energy level is as you leave them. Did being with them drain your energy, or top it up? Are you feeling more energised, or less?

So a sale is really nothing more than a five-step transfer of energy:

1. You feel happy.

2. You make your customer feel great (using the advanced subliminal communication skills in this book).

3. You make your customer feel great about your product (again, using the skills in this book).

4. You make the sale.

5. Your customer now feels happy.

* * *

I am going to great lengths to hammer this point home for you because this is the secret to sales success.

(It also happens to be the secret to a long and happy life full of joy and great relationships and unending adventure, enjoyment, wealth and, of course, fabulous sex. But let's not digress!)

You see, there is only one reason that I wrote this book, and it is also why I love teaching this material in my live "Power Selling" seminars and workshops.

When I set out, I thought: "Who needs another sales course? There are already so many other wonderful sales courses around and so many talented sales trainers who teach fantastic sales skills." But then I looked closer, and I realised there is a big problem with almost all of them.

Just about every corporate sales training course on the market makes one fundamental error, which is not surprising because it is a terribly easy one to make and most people make it every day of their lives without ever realising they are doing it.

It is also why, with all this wealth of knowledge available to you, there are still so many frustrated sales people out there who just aren't getting the results they want – not just in sales, but in every area of their lives.

The problem is these courses set out to teach you all these amazing skills so you make more sales, which will make you more money, which will make you feel good.

"What's wrong with that?" you may ask.

No, really... what IS wrong with that?

Yes, it's backwards, isn't it? It's completely the wrong way round.

The truth is, when you start out feeling good you are going to be 10 times more effective in whatever you do, which means you will make 10 times as many sales – and therefore make 10 times as much money.

So now you're feeling even better, which means you will perform even better, so you will make even more sales... and so on.

* * *

Think about this. Please don't just take my word for it. In fact, throughout this book I urge you to question everything you read to make sure you agree with it and really install it in your mind at the deepest level.

You see, if all those sales systems out there really worked, everyone would be making truckloads of money and be happy.

But they're not, are they?

Ironically, that is precisely why there are so many sales teachers around, all offering excellent sales skills – and not just in seminars either. The bookshelves are also stacked with all kinds of magic sales systems that are "guaranteed" to make you money – and therefore to make you happy.

The fact is, if those systems actually worked almost all the sales gurus would go out of business overnight because you'd only need to read one sales book or attend one sales seminar and you'd be sorted.

No, there are so many of them precisely because they don't work. People go from one to another looking for an answer that isn't there, so there is a constant itch that none of the books can scratch – which generates even more books as people keep searching.

Meanwhile, all those salespeople out there find they enjoy some level of success with their new skills, but pretty soon they hit a wall because they have not learned how to manage their emotional state on a daily basis.

Before long they become frustrated and unhappy and have to drag themselves out of bed every morning thinking: "God, why do I have to go to work!"

They have no idea how to make themselves feel good because their happiness is conditional on being able to succeed in order to feel happy, rather than the other way round.

* * *

So now you're probably sitting there thinking, "Well, that's great, Simon. That's all very well in theory. But how can I feel good on a daily basis? How can I feel good when I'm struggling to make my monthly targets, or my boss is a bastard, or it's raining, or the car won't start, or I've just had a fight with my girlfriend, boyfriend, spouse, dog, or whoever?"

In other words, you want to know: "How can I be happy all the time, no matter what?"

Well, that's the $64 squillion dollar question, isn't it?

That's the answer everyone is searching for.

It's the reason God invented mountain tops.

Well, you'll be relieved – and delighted – to know that at no extra charge I'll be giving you the answer to this question too when I show you how to literally *condition* yourself to feel great on a regular basis by controlling what you focus on with your mind and how you move your body to give you massive amounts of energy at a moment's notice.

Yes, of course you will also learn how to make sales smoothly and easily,.. and have tonnes of fun in the process. We'll get to the skills section of the sales course in Chapter 3. But the focus of these first few chapters is on feeling good, because if you don't get THIS right, nothing else you will ever learn – in this book or any other – is ever going to give you what you are looking for: namely happiness, fulfillment, joy and connection, as well as fast cars, shoes make-up, great clothes and all that other important stuff!

* * *

Selling is the best job in the world

The first crucial step in feeling good when it comes to sales is to make sure you have the right perception of what selling is.

Sadly, most people's perception of sales – and sales people – is not always a positive one. But I am doing everything in my power to change that, and I need your help. So let's start with YOU.

Please find four or five cards and write on them in very large letters these words:

"I am an Agent of Happiness."

Stick the cards up on your bathroom mirror at home, in your car, and on your computer at work to remind you who you truly are.

(Don't worry if your colleagues laugh at you. They will soon stop laughing when they see the results that you are getting!)

And you thought you were just a sales person? Hah! No, no, no, no, no. That's the old perception. As of this moment, you are now officially an Agent of Happiness.

I want you to forget all the negative social conditioning that has sadly been attached to the words "sales" and "salesman" or "saleswoman", and instead focus on all that is amazing about this wonderful business we are in.

It's true that some sales professionals over the years have abused the trust of customers in order to make a fast buck, and that this has justifiably created a natural suspicion of sales people in the perception of the public. But they are not us, are they? And all the information that I am going to teach you here in this book would turn to dust in their hands if they tried to use it.

The truth is, selling is absolutely the best job in the world. Not only do we have the potential to earn enormous amounts of money and have heaps of fun in the process, but we also have the opportunity to improve other people's lives on a daily basis.

People say money doesn't buy happiness, but they obviously just don't know where to shop. Money absolutely does buy temporary happiness in the form of pleasure. The saying is incomplete. What it should say is "Money doesn't buy LASTING happiness."

Almost everything in people's lives that gives them pleasure has been sold to them at one time or another: their home, their car, their wedding dress, their engagement ring, anniversary presents, clothes, food, holidays, furniture, even their knowledge through books and college and seminars. And now with internet dating, yes even love can be sold to them.

And then when they go into business we are able to sell them pleasure there too: advertising to grow their sales, office equipment to improve their efficiency, mobile phone plans to save them money, insurance for their peace of mind, and so on.

* * *

So to sum all of this up in one sentence: you are in the business of making people happy.

And what you are going to learn in this book will make you very, very good at it!

PART ONE:

CONTACT

Step 1:
Get ready...

Prepare. Prepare. Prepare.

THE first step to sales excellence, like the first step of all journeys, is the simplest yet also the most important. As with anything in life – from throwing a party, to going to a job interview, to playing a sport – the more time and effort you spend preparing, the better your results will be.

* * *

There are five key areas of preparation that you need to focus on:

1. Know your product

You must know all the benefits and shortcomings of your product off by heart and inside out or you will appear unprofessional and may flounder later on when you are in front of the customer and they are firing questions at you.

You will also need to know as much as you can about your competitors' products and how yours compare with theirs.

Note:

In front of a customer, never talk badly about your competitors. Say they have some great products... but yours are better. And certainly never criticise a product that the customer already owns. You will make them feel stupid for making a bad purchase, and no one likes to be made to feel stupid. You can kiss goodbye to rapport.

So instead, say something like: *"Yes, that certainly was a good machine when it came out, but sadly it is quite outdated now and there are many things it can't do."*

* * *

Please do your homework on this first step. There are no short cuts, but your preparation will pay big dividends when you get out into the field.

2. Know your prospect

People are impressed when you can show them you have taken the time to find out what they do and how they do it. It tells them you are taking a genuine interest in their business and are not just gunning for a quick sale.

All companies have a website these days, so take some time to read about the company, when it was founded, what it does, and the key people.

Then make sure you drop this information into your conversation early on to impress them. Not too much, just one or two facts to show you have bothered to do your homework.

3. Know what you are going to say

Have your telephone scripts ready to consult if you need to. I will be giving you some great ideas for what to say in Chapter 3. The more you can memorise them, the less your words will sound like a script and the better you will be able flow with the conversation as it unfolds.

4. Get a wireless telephone headset

You will need to have both of your hands free when you talk on the telephone. I will explain why in more detail in Chapter 3.

For now, please just be aware that it is absolutely ESSENTIAL that you have a wireless headset so you are able to move around and gesticulate when you are talking on the phone with your prospective customers. I can't emphasise strongly enough how important this is!

5. Answer their questions upfront

There are seven key questions that every prospect will have on their mind. Have good answers prepared and memorised for all of them in advance:

1. What is it?
2. What's in it for me?
3. Will it give me what I want?
4. What does it cost?
5. Will it be worth it?
6. What do (or will) other people say about it?
7. Do I really need it NOW?

Step 2:
Get set...

Put yourself in a peak state and have no fear

C AN you remember a time when you were absolutely involved in what you were doing? When you were so focused on a task and were so "in the moment" that you performed at 100 per cent of your capability?

Athletes and actors achieve this, don't they? And so do top salespeople. This is the "in-flow" state when relationships are built and sales are made, because when you are completely focused on the person you are talking to, you are able to exert a powerful influence on them.

This chapter deals with the two main ways to put yourself in a peak state before making a phone call or a sales presentation:

1. Your mental focus.

2. Your physical energy levels.

It will also show you how to eradicate the two major obstacles that prevent us from staying in a peak state and operating at our most-effective best: the dreaded fear of failure and fear of rejection.

1. Control your focus

It's true, isn't it, that whatever we focus on, we experience. In other words, if we focus on all that's wrong with our life we are going to feel lousy. And if we focus on all that's great in our life we will feel empowered and motivated to make it even better.

A good analogy is to imagine you are driving in your car and you come to a corner too fast. If you turn your head and look round the corner, you will most likely steer round the corner and stay on the road. But if you fixate your gaze on the tree right in front of you and say to yourself "Don't hit the tree! I mustn't hit the tree!" Guess what? You're going to hit the tree.

Our brain doesn't hear the "don't" or the "mustn't". It just hears "hit the tree".

To convince you of this, please read this sentence: "Don't think of a pink elephant."

What are you picturing in your mind right now?

Exercise

Look around the room you are sitting in and notice everything in it that's a particular colour. Blue, say, or red or yellow. As you look closely you will see objects you haven't noticed for ages, despite the fact that they have been right there in the room all along.

* * *

The power of questions

What we focus on is primarily guided by the questions we ask ourselves. In fact, I would go so far as to say that the quality of our life is based almost entirely on the quality of the questions we ask ourselves on a regular basis.

Our brain is like a computer that is hotwired to automatically answer any question we ask of it. So if we ask ourselves poor questions such as "Why does this always happen to me?" our brain – which doesn't understand the concept of a rhetorical question – has to give us an answer.

And because this question is so negative, our brain will come back with something equally negative, such as:

"Because you're a goose." Or:

"Because all people are bastards." Or even worse:

"Because you don't deserve any better."

Negative questions are guaranteed to give us negative answers, which in turn are guaranteed to put us in a lousy state of mind. We need to be in a great state to be effective – in sales, and in life – so one of the most valuable changes you will ever make in your life is to learn to ask yourself empowering questions.

Some examples of empowering questions when faced with adversity or a disappointing result might be:

"How can I turn this around?"

"What can I learn from this experience?"

"What's great about this that I haven't noticed yet?"

"How can I get this handled… and ENJOY the process?"

* * *

Morning questions

Get into the habit of asking yourself empowering questions when you first wake up in the morning to put yourself in a great state for the day and focused on all the wondrous possibilities that the day holds for you.

"What am I happiest about in my life right now?"

"What am I most grateful for in my life right now?"

"What am I most excited about?"

"Who loves me, and who do I love? And how does that make me feel?"

"What can I do today that I have never done before?"

Write them down and stick them up on your bathroom mirror. Do them daily when you first wake up and brush your teeth for a full two minutes.

And don't just run through them quickly as though they are a chore. Really stop and think about the questions – and FEEL the answers that your brain provides. It's vital that you FULLY ASSOCIATE yourself to the pleasure these answers make you feel.

* * *

2. Move your body

The second way to change the way you are feeling and put yourself in a peak state is to change your physiology; in other words, change the way you sit, stand and move.

This is by far the quickest way to put yourself into a great state of mind by sending massive amounts of energy coursing through your body.

It is extremely difficult to feel depressed when you stand up tall with your shoulders back, arms outstretched and put a big silly grin on your face.

Try it now...

Stand up as you read. Put your shoulders back. Look up at the ceiling. Now raise your arms out wide and put a big silly grin on your face. Stay like that. Keep smiling and laughing... and now just try to feel depressed!

OK. Stay standing like that and in a moment – but not yet – I'm going to ask you to bring your arms together in a rush of explosive energy and clap your hands and then punch the air with your fist and say with all the passion you can muster: "YES."

Ready? And... GO!

And again... "YES!!"

And again one more time... "YESSSSS!!!"

Excellent.

You have just created what Tony Robbins calls a "Power Move" – a sudden explosive gesture that can transform you from feeling lethargic or worse into feeling absolutely unstoppable in a millisecond.

So I have a question for you: how are you feeling now? Notice how alert you are and how much energy you have.

Good job.

OK, you can go ahead and sit back down, but still with tonnes of energy in your body.

* * *

As you sit there feeling more energised and more alive than you felt before, I have some more questions for you:

– Would this be a good way to feel before you pick up the phone?

– Do you think you would have more of your personal power at your disposal if you felt like this before making a sales pitch?

– Would you be more likely to make a sale or persuade someone it would be worthwhile hearing what you have to offer them if you felt like this?

Athletes do this, don't they? You've seen the long-jumpers and pole-vaulters at the Olympics getting the crowd to cheer and clap before they start their run.

Please use this every time you feel you need to boost your energy levels: by your desk before making a call; in the lift or toilet before making a sales presentation. Any time you feel sluggish or ineffectual, you can fire off your Power Move and instantly put yourself in a peak state.

Remember, the way we move our body creates the emotions we feel at any given moment. The clue is right there in the word "emotion". It is literally e-motion. Our motion determines our emotion.

* * *

3. Conquer your fears

Now you know how to feel great instantly, but there is something that can make you feel lousy again just as quickly, isn't there?

That's right... the dreaded FEAR.

Please write this out on a card and put it up above your desk: "WHAT WOULD YOU DO IF YOU KNEW YOU COULD NOT FAIL?"

This is the best question you can ever ask yourself because the answer is, of course, anything you want to.

You see, FEAR – which stands for False Evidence Appearing Real – is an illusion. If we are afraid of something, it is simply because we don't fully understand it yet.

Isn't it true that when you face a fear head on it usually goes away, and you are left wondering what you were so afraid about?

So let's once and for all seek out and destroy the two most common causes of call avoidance: the "Evil Twins" – fear of failure and fear of rejection.

In fact, in this case they are really one and the same thing, aren't they? If your prospective customer rejects your offer, you may feel that you have "failed" in your outcome which was to get them to accept your offer.

But is one customer saying no to you really a failure?

Is 10 customers saying no to you really a failure?

The answer is it is if you believe it is, and it isn't if you believe it isn't.

I know that sounds a bit like psycho-babble, but the truth is there is actually no such thing in life as "failure" or "success", only results.

Neither success nor failure can be qualified in any way that is measurable. Ask one person how much money they would have to earn to feel like a success, and they might say $50 million. Ask the person next to them and they might say $250,000 a year. Ask a third and they might say that no amount of money can make them feel successful because they measure success in their life by the level of love they feel from their family and friends.

The truth is, success and failure are what you decide they are. Remember, in life there are only results. Whether you choose to qualify a result as a "success" or a "failure" is up to you. And your decision will be based purely on the beliefs you hold about failure and success.

The sad thing is most of us have chosen (or inherited from our parents) beliefs that make it extremely easy for us to feel as though we have "failed" and extremely difficult for us to feel we have "succeeded".

If you have a belief that says, "Unless I close nine out of every 10 customers I call then I have failed", that will be true for you. It will also guarantee you will feel like a failure almost all the time.

Exercise

Please take a moment to write down what has to happen for you to feel as though you have failed. In other words, what beliefs do you currently have that determine whether an outcome is a "success" or a "failure"?

<u>Examples:</u>

"If they reject my proposal, I have failed."

"If I don't get the sale, I have failed."

"If I don't make $20K a month, I have failed."

"If the outcome doesn't turn out exactly as I wanted it to, then I have failed."

"In order to feel like a success I have to be earning "X" number of dollars a year."

"In order to feel like I have really succeeded, I must be the No.1 sales person in the company / the world / the universe."

Now look closely at the beliefs you have written down and decide if you have made it easy or difficult for you to feel like you have failed.

Also, have you made it easy or difficult to feel that you have succeeded?

Wouldn't it be great if you could literally reprogram yourself to make it very easy for you to feel successful and extremely difficult – or even impossible – to feel like you have failed?

Would that help you in making calls?

Would that make you more effective, not just in business but in every area of your life?

Well, the good news is it's ridiculously easy to do just that!

* * *

Let's take another look at the beliefs you have written down. How can we change these so that you almost never feel like you have failed and you almost always feel that you are succeeding?

Now let's think up some new beliefs that make it easy to feel like a success and virtually impossible to feel like a failure.

<u>Examples:</u>

"As long as I learn something from the experience then it was a success."

"The only way I can ever fail is if I don't try."

"I am succeeding if I am above ground."

"I am a success because I am a good person."

"I can only be rejected if I act dishonestly, and I would reject myself if I ever did that."

Please create your own list of new and empowering beliefs, write them on a card and put them up on your mirror next to your Morning Questions.

Spend a minute or two each morning conditioning yourself to think this way until these new beliefs are installed in the deepest level of your brain.

Do this every day for a month (the time it takes for a new habit to be formed) and you will be not only a positive, energised and unstoppable influencer – but a fearless one as well.

Step 3:
Call!

Get past the gatekeeper and make the appointment

WHEN using the telephone as a marketing tool, your objective is not coercion, but influence. Influence allows you to cause an effect without the direct use of force.

We are influencing each other all the time, aren't we? Every time you smile at someone, for example, you cause them to like you.

When people interact face to face, they exercise three types of influence:

– Our words convey 7% of our influence.

– Our voice qualities carry 38% of our influence.

– Our body language shouts 55% of our influence.

But on the phone this changes radically. All that body language is screened out, leaving us with less than half of our influencing powers.

On the phone our voice qualities convey a massive 86 per cent of influence. The words we use are now twice as important, but they still account for a tiny 14 per cent.

This takes an enormous amount of pressure off our telephone sales scripts, doesn't it?

Words are certainly still important, but far more important is our "voice quality" – in other words, how we sound to our prospective customer.

Voice quality is a combination of:
– Tone
– Pace
– Pitch
– Volume
– Vocal variety

So now you understand why it is absolutely essential to use a headset so that you can stand up and walk around and gesticulate, exactly as you would if you were talking face to face. Trust me, the customer will hear the difference in your voice.

Some top sales people I know even put a mirror on the wall so that they can look at themselves and smile as though they are talking to the customer face to face.

Again, you can be sure that when you are smiling the customer will hear it in your voice.

Sit UP, not down

It is very hard to sound passionate when you are sitting slumped over a desk. That is why I always stand up and walk around when I make important phone calls.

If you must sit, sit up straight in your chair with lots of energy. Clap your hands, lift your head up and smile before making the call.

The power of belief

The most important quality in your voice is actually not a physiological one, but an emotional one. It is your level of belief in what you are selling.

Influence is assured if you truly believe that what you are giving is much more valuable than what you are asking for in return. So the next step in using the telephone effectively is to have a firm belief that what you are offering is of great value to your customer.

I would suggest that if you feel you are unable to achieve this due to the nature of your product, consider changing jobs now. If you believe in what you are selling, you will not only be much happier, you will be infinitely more effective… and make much more money too.

Be a giver, not a taker

Before each and every phone call, take a moment to see yourself as a giver, not a taker. Really FEEL it and

BELIEVE it. Know in your heart and in your gut that you are giving much more value than you would ever expect to receive in return.

Come from this frame, and watch your sales soar.

* * *

Find the decision-maker

You must, must, MUST make sure that the person you are going to talk to is the person who has the power to decide whether or not to buy. Otherwise you are wasting everybody's time, including yours.

How do you find them? Simple. Just ring the switchboard and ask them who it is (using your friendliest voice).

Explain you want to write them a letter, which is not a lie (please NEVER lie – karma hurts like hell!) because one day you will need to send them something – be it a receipt, an invoice, a product update, or whatever.

Then ask for the name of the decision-maker's personal assistant. Get the correct spelling for both of them, and the correct title of the decision-maker. Then, as a casual afterthought, and just before hanging up, say to the switchboard operator:

"Actually, I might just have a quick chat with them now. Can you please put me through to (the name of the assistant)*?"*

If the switchboard doesn't know who the decision-maker is, ask to be put through to the Office Manager (get their name first) and ask them. They will tell you who to talk to (again get names and titles), or else if they are the person who makes the purchasing decisions then you have arrived at the right place.

* * *

Make the appointment

When you are put through, you will probably get the personal assistant, the dreaded "gatekeeper". But worry not because you now know their name (James Smith for this example) and the name of their boss (let's say she's called Mary Jones).

In my experience, the best tactic is to be incredibly upbeat, chatty and friendly and say:

"Hi James, it's Simon from XYZ. Is Mary there?"

They will often put you straight through, thinking you are a friend of their boss. And no PA wants to risk offending a friend of their boss.

If they do put you straight through, be aware that the boss may be a little disgruntled so it is important to praise James and make Mary realise that it was not his fault. It wouldn't be fair on James if he got into trouble, and besides you need the gatekeeper on your side for future calls.

So first up tell Mary who you are, what company you work for and why you are calling. You must ALWAYS do this with every call anyway. And in this case, if your gambit has worked, you must also answer the question in her mind of how you got through to her.

"Hi Mary, this is Simon Firth from XYZ. I must start by saying that your assistant James is very kind and extremely efficient and I think he thought I was someone else. Please forgive him (laugh)... *and please forgive me too for the interruption. I just wanted to very quickly ask you when was the last time someone from XYZ called you to update you on our newest range of money-saving widgets?"*

Let them answer, and as they do listen very closely to their tone of voice to quickly gauge two things:

1. Their mood.

2. The tone, volume and speed with which they talk, so you can match them exactly and start creating rapport immediately (more on this in Chapter 4).

This is a great opening question because you are not asking the customer whether they are interested or not, only when was the last time someone from your company called. Whether they say never, or a long time ago, you can now get straight to the point.

Remember, your phone call is an unwelcome interruption so your goal is to make an appointment and get off the phone as quickly as possible. Therefore you need to cut to the chase immediately.

"Great. Well in your opinion when would be a perfect time for me to come and see you? Sometime tomorrow morning, or later in the week?"

Note:

The "in your opinion" frame is a powerful subliminal tool because in their subconscious mind you are not actually asking them for anything, merely their opinion. It makes the question seem harmless and much easier for them to answer.

Also, you need to use what is known as a "Double Bind" question whereby you give them two choices, both of which you are happy with because you tricked them into forgetting they have a third choice... which is to say "not interested". (More on this on page 130).

– If they choose tomorrow, use the Double Bind structure again by saying: *"Fantastic. Which is better for you, 10 or 11?"*

– If they choose later in the week, say: *"Fantastic. Which is better for you, Wednesday or Thursday?"* (Try and avoid Fridays. Nothing ever gets done on a Friday.)

– Whichever day they choose, say: *"Perfect. Which time is best for you, 10 or 11?"* (Always try for the morning as people are much more productive before lunch.)

– When you confirm the time, say: *"Excellent. Thank you so much for your time. I'll see you then."* And hang up. Job well done.

* * *

What if the gatekeeper is difficult?

If the "friends gambit" didn't work with the gatekeeper and they ask you what you are calling about, stay friendly and be vague:

"Oh, it's regarding your phone account/printing account/car fleet account" (depending on what it is you are selling).

If that still doesn't work, you need to sell them with:

"It's just a regular courtesy call to update Mary on some of our latest widgets. I'm so sorry, James, I was supposed to ring Mary a while ago but we have been so busy. I hope she is not cross that I haven't called her sooner."

This response is designed to re-frame the gatekeeper into thinking that his boss actually wanted you to call – and in fact has been WAITING for you to call. It doesn't always work, but I have got through on many occasions using this gambit.

If James says Mary is busy, NEVER leave a phone message (I'll explain why at the end of this chapter). Instead, use the Double Bind to ask for a good time to call again: *"In about half an hour, or later this morning?"*

If James starts to get all protective of Mary and says something like: "Thank you but we're not interested", whatever you do don't fight him. You need to try to make friends with him at this point.

Try one more approach, with absolute sincerity and a touch of charm in your voice. Remember, most PAs don't really like their boss all that much and are only protecting them so they don't get into trouble.

Laugh and say: *"Wow, James, I'm impressed. I hope Mary appreciates the amazing job you do in protecting her from all us horrible sales people. I receive a lot of sales calls too and I could really use someone like you."*

Laugh again. Then add: *"I don't know what she's paying you, but how about I double it and you come and work WITH (not "for") me?"*

If the joke works, keep up the banter for a while to build rapport, then say:

"I have to tell you that I'm actually NOT a horrible sales person and I do passionately believe that Mary will be interested in what I have to offer her. But I also know she's extremely busy and would quite possibly be cross with you if you put me through to her right now. And you have been so kind that I definitely don't want

that to happen to you. So how about I just mail you our brochures and you can show them to her for me at your convenience? Would that be OK with you?"

James will almost certainly say yes to that. But you don't send the brochures to him. You drop them round to him later that day – or the next day at the very latest – so you can meet him.

He will remember your conversation and you should be able to continue your great rapport in person. Tell him you were seeing a client down the street and thought you'd just pop in quickly to say hi *"because you were so nice on the phone that I really wanted to meet you"*.

Then ask him if it would be possible to have just three minutes of Mary's time now that you are there, and then sit and wait, making chit-chat.

By now James is probably more on your side than Mary's and hopefully will get you in to see her.

* * *

To rewind for a second, if James didn't respond to your charm offensive on the phone, simply move on to the next name on your list. Remember, sales is a numbers game. And the key word is: "NEXT."

However, if he did put you through to Mary after finding out why you were calling, say this to her:

"Hi Mary, this is Simon Firth from XYZ. Thank you so much for taking my call. I know you are very busy and I apologise for the interruption. I am just calling to ask you when was the last time someone from XYZ contacted you to update you on our newest range of money-saving widgets?"

Again, as before, this is a great opening question because it allows you to gauge Mary's mood and voice qualities while she answers it. You can then adjust what you say next – and how you say it – accordingly.

– If Mary is interested, make an appointment to come in and see her using the Double Bind and get off the phone as soon as possible.

– If she is not interested, agree with her. (Never disagree with anything a customer says... EVER.)

"I understand. Of course you're not interested. How could you be? You have far too many demands on your time to stay up to date on all the latest advances and money-saving deals. But if you were to give me just 10 minutes of your time – not now, obviously, but AT A TIME OF YOUR CHOOSING – I feel certain I could show you some money-saving solutions that WOULD be of interest to you. Would that be OK?"

If she bites, make the appointment as above. If she resists, persist. People say no as a knee-jerk reaction. You need to take at least FOUR nos before hanging up.

This time you need to be very polite and push gently: *"I apologise and I certainly mean no disrespect because I know how busy you are. I just have a very short proposal that I want to share with you, and it's obvious that you don't want to hear about it now. But if you did want to hear about it, when would be a good time for you?"*

If she says yes, make the appointment using the Double Bind. If you get a third no, align with her and use humour and passion:

"I completely understand. (Laugh.) In fact, many of my happiest customers told me to go away far less politely than you at first – and they are now very grateful that I was so persistent.

"I assure you the only reason I am being so persistent with you is that I am absolutely PASSIONATE about what I do – and I know in my heart that our newest-model widgets can really help you and your business.

"I don't want to take up any more of your time, so (not "but") *can I quickly suggest a proposal that might be perfect for you?"*

Don't let her answer. Move quickly on to surprise her with a totally unexpected and yet harmless question.

"Do you drink coffee?"

Now let her answer. If she says "Sorry?" or "What did you say?" repeat the question exactly – and then shut up. Wait for her to answer. She will not have been expecting this question and will probably answer "Yes" automatically. (If she says no, try tea. And then juice.)

"Great. Then I'm sure that at some time in your hectic day you normally take 10 minutes out to get a coffee/tea/juice – I'm guessing maybe mid-morning? Well, how about I come in at the EXACT time that you have your break and spend just NINE minutes running very quickly through what XYZ can offer you and your business, and I will be out of your hair well before you've finished your coffee/tea/juice. Wouldn't that be the perfect way for you to find out if we can help you without taking up any of your work time?"

If you get a fourth no, or she is still wavering, go to your final gambit. Laugh and say:

"OK, I was hoping it didn't have to come to this, but a couple of my regular customers have taken me up on this challenge – and I'm sure you'll find it just as much FUN as they did.

"I would like to promise you that if I take up one second more than nine minutes of your time I will personally donate $500 to the charity of your choice.

"That way, even if I can't interest you – and I know I can – I'll have wasted none of your work time... and BEST OF ALL some needy people who are much less fortunate than us will have a great day.

"Don't you agree that would be worth just nine minutes of OUR (not "your") time?"

She will find it extremely difficult to say no to that. You can even explain that so far you have never had to part with $500, but perhaps she can be the first if she can make you run over time. Set her a friendly challenge.

* * *

Look what you have done with this approach!

Instead of being grumpy at the prospect of another dreary sales pitch, Mary now has a fun challenge to look forward to. She will probably tell her colleagues about it – and maybe even her husband as she leaves for work on the morning of your appointment.

Above all, she will be looking forward to a sales pitch probably for the first time in her life.

If this works, make the appointment, again using the Double Bind. If it doesn't, move on to the next call knowing you tried your best.

* * *

Now, here's the clincher of this fun and original approach. Just before you hang up, you say: *"Oh, by the way, Mary, how do you have your coffee?"*

Write down the answer so you remember it and get it right, then say: *"Great. Same as me. I know a wonderful little coffee shop not far from your office. I'll pick us up a couple of cappuccinos on the way in."*

If she tries to refuse your offer, interrupt her kindly by saying: *"Thank you, Mary, you are very kind – but I insist on it. It's the least I can do after you have been so generous in agreeing to see me. I'll see you at 11am tomorrow. Looking forward to it."*

And hang up.

Not only has no other sales person ever done this to Mary, but she is now starting to think of you as a friend. Also, you have invoked the Law of Reciprocation, which states that when you give someone something, however small, they feel compelled to give you something back – in this case hopefully a big, juicy contract in exchange for the price of a cup of coffee.

* * *

Important notes about this approach

– Prepare an eight-minute presentation in which you grab the client's interest by making big claims about what your products can do and how they can save them money (this is explained in detail in Chapter 5). Highlight the features of each product very quickly and focus on the cost-saving and quality factors.

– When you arrive for the meeting, take out of your briefcase one of those big, colourful old-fashioned alarm clocks with two big bells on top and place it on the customer's desk.

This is going to make them laugh and create great rapport. Set the alarm clock and start your presentation.

– After eight and a half minutes, start packing up and ask them if they would like to try your product for free for a trial period, no questions asked, or if they would like you to stay longer so you can explain in more detail all the amazing benefits they are going to enjoy.

If they ask you to stay, turn off the alarm clock and put it back in your briefcase. Now the deal is off and you can give them your full presentation. But before you do, ask them with a big smile on your face:

"By the way, what IS your favourite charity? Really? That's one of my favourites too. It's a great cause. I've got an idea – let's agree that when (not "if") *we finalise the deal, let's both kick in an extra $50 or $100 each and give it to them anyway. Wouldn't that be great? It is tax-deductible after all."*

The client is going to realise that you are the real deal and you weren't just exploiting the underprivileged to get your foot in the door. You have now earned their admiration and their trust, and you have also helped the needy in the process.

So the customer feels great. You feel great. And after all, what's $50 or $100 out of their company's money — and out of your big, fat juicy commission?

Now, that's taking sales to a whole new level!

Don't you agree?

* * *

Four quick points about using the phone:

1. Every phone call is an interruption

Every time you call someone you are interrupting what they are doing. Always come from this frame of mind and soothe their annoyance by telling them right up front that this interruption will be worth their while.

2. Say who you are and why you are calling

Start every call like this. You sound professional by getting straight to the point, plus these questions will be on their mind and you want to answer them right away.

3. Always ask permission on a mobile

If calling someone on their mobile, start by saying who you are and then ask right away if they are able to talk. If they say no, ask them when would be a good time. Use the Double Bind by giving them two options: *"Shall I call back in a few minutes, or later this morning/afternoon?"*

4. Never leave a message

Always say you will call back, and try and find out a good time to call. If you leave a message you give away all your power. If they do call back, you won't be ready. And if they don't, when you call again they already know who you are and now you appear an annoyance.

PART TWO:

CONNECT

Step 4:
Make them love you...

Create rapport and align with them

BEFORE we even start on how to create instant and lasting rapport with your customer or client, please, please PLEASE make sure that your mobile phone is turned off or on silent while you are with them.

Nothing shatters rapport faster than your phone going off in the middle of a presentation.

Is it switched off?

Good. Then let's begin.

* * *

What sort of a sales person are you?

That may sound like a strange question to start this chapter about creating rapport with your customers, but it goes to the heart of everything this book stands for, everything I stand for... and everything I know that you stand for as well.

Your goal is to make them your friend

– You are not trying to outwit your customer.

– You are not trying to trick them.

– You are not trying to coerce them.

– You are not trying to "get one over them".

– You are not trying to sell them anything they don't genuinely want to have.

– You are on their side.

– You are trying to make them your friend so that you can improve their life with the product or service you are offering.

Remember this:

The most successful salespeople are those who have made the most friends.

* * *

To make someone your friend, you will need to do two things:

1. You must make them believe you are like them by creating rapport, and I'm about to give you SEVEN ways to create lasting rapport with everyone you meet.

2. You must discover what their values are – in other words, what is most important to them – so you can make sure you and your product are in alignment with them.

Let's start with rapport.

* * *

1. Seven steps to create rapport

It's the oldest – and truest – cliche in the world of sales that the customer buys YOU before they buy what you are offering. So you must make them love you.

This is one of the most important of all the 10 steps to being a sales superstar, and I am going to spend quite a bit of time on it.

If you get this step right, everything else will flow easily from here. If you don't get it right, you are going to find it extremely difficult to sell anything to anyone.

Step 1: Be enthusiastic

Right from the start, use masses of enthusiasm and passion to engage them and make them excited.

A sale is not just a transfer of money; it is a transfer of enthusiasm.

Think back to the last time you bought something off a salesperson and thoroughly enjoyed the process.

Isn't it true that both of you built up your enthusiasm about how great you were going to look in the dress or the suit or the sunglasses, or whatever it was, and you fed off each other's enthusiasm?

If you had been enthusiastic and the salesperson wasn't, would you have felt so good? Of course not.

So what is enthusiasm? Yes, it is being cheerful and upbeat. But it's actually something more important – and more infectious – than that.

Enthusiasm is a sincere belief in the value of your product. You must sincerely believe that the product you are offering will dramatically improve the quality of your customer's life, no matter whether you are selling houses, cars, office printers, phones or advertising space.

You can't fake this bit.

If you are serious about sales and you are selling a product or service you don't believe in, leave now and find a job where you do believe in what you are selling.

I am sorry if this bothers you. Yes, it will be a short-term upheaval – but the benefits in the long run will be more than worth it. I promise you.

Step 2. Make a great first impression

People tend to make up their minds about whether they like someone or not almost as soon as they meet them. Having a great handshake is one of the best ways to make a great impression right from the start. Here's how to do the perfect "two-handed handshake":

– Reach out your right hand enthusiastically and, as they take it, close your right hand firmly but not too hard in theirs.

– Keep your right hand vertical.

– Then immediately reach out your left hand and close it gently around their right wrist to give them a two-handed handshake.

– The duration of the perfect handshake is two seconds, no more and no less.

By using both hands you are subliminally demonstrating much more commitment to meeting them than if you were to use just one hand. All the while you should be looking them straight in the eye with a warm smile (smile with your eyes, not just your mouth) and saying: *"Thank you so much for seeing me. I am VERY pleased to meet you."*

Step 3. Use questions, humour and compliments

<u>Questions:</u>

As we have already seen, you need to be bubbling over with enthusiasm, but not so much that you are annoying. If they are feeling flat and you come in at a million miles an hour, all you are going to succeed in doing is pissing them off.

So to start with you need to match your energy levels to theirs. And the best way to find out where they are at is to ask them a harmless but probing question, such as:

"How's your morning going so far?"

If bad, smile and say softly: *"I'm sorry to hear that."* Then raise the tempo a little bit by saying: *"Well, hopefully I can help make it better."*

If good, take them even higher with: *"Well, it's about to get even better."*

Humour:

Now that you have used your opening question or questions to find out how they are feeling you can move straight on to use humour and compliments to make them feel better than they did before you arrived.

Remember, your goal is to make them feel better than they did before you came in so that they will associate you with feeling good.

If you are doing your nine-minute pitch from Chapter 3, the funny alarm clock will work perfectly for the humour. If not, use an amusing opening line to make them smile:

"It's actually very funny. I've been running late all day because my son threw up on my suit just as I was leaving home.

He has a knack for doing that before I see a really important client. Does that ever happen to you?"

This allows you to talk about a point of common interest. If you don't have kids, say your dog drooled on your suit. If you don't have a dog, say your wife / husband / housemate spilt their porridge.

You have broken the ice. And best of all, you have subtly told them that they are a really important client – and that alone will create rapport.

The Three-Step Compliment:

The secret to a great compliment lies in three steps, not just one.

Step 1: Give them the compliment.

Step 2: Explain why you like whatever it is you are praising.

Step 3: Finish by asking them a question about it to reinforce your interest and to allow them to talk about whatever it is you are praising.

Example:

"That's a fantastic painting. I've been looking for one just like that for my office for ages. Where did you get it?"

Step 4. Match them

When talking with people, whether it's on the phone or face to face, it is important to be as much like the person you are talking to as you can.

People like people who are just like them, and they don't like people with whom they have little or nothing in common.

Have you ever found yourself growing impatient when someone speaks too softly, or too loudly, or talks too slowly, or jabbers away at a million miles an hour? The fact is, we are most comfortable with someone who speaks at our own pace and volume.

So to create a comfort zone for your customer, try to mirror exactly the pace and volume at which they talk.

And to make them really warm to you, try to match their vocabulary by using their buzz words and phrases – although obviously don't overdo it.

Note:

In order to be able to do this effectively, you need to develop what is known as "Sensory Acuity" to notice all the little details about a person, including the way they speak, the words they use, what they are wearing, the way they move etc.

Sensory Acuity is quite simply the single most important sales skill you will ever develop.

Learn to pay attention to everything around you. Have your "antennae" up at all times. Notice their expressions, tone of voice, vocabulary, body language, energy changes, their mood, their shoes, their office decor. Is their desk neat or messy? What photos are they displaying? What does their hairstyle say about them? The phrases they use? Their jewellery? Their watch? Their tie?

Also, listen to all the verbal clues they will give you. And notice immediately when they start to drift or lose interest and adjust yourself, your energy levels and the words you say accordingly to match them again.

* * *

One of the best ways to match your customer and make them feel that you are just like them is to establish whether they are primarily Visual, Auditory or Kinesthetic (feelings) in the way they sort information – and adjust your words and energy to match theirs.

Most of us have all three qualities but we tend to have one primary one, and that is the one you are after.

As you will see, it is absolutely crucial that you ascertain your prospect's VAK strategy because if, for example, you try to sell a Visual in the same way you sell an Auditory or a Kinesthetic, you will bump up against a brick wall of resistance. And you won't even know why!

Visual people

Visual people make purchasing decisions based on how something LOOKS to them, or how it will make them look. They will often decide to buy for emotional reasons and then seek to justify their decision with rational reasons.

They use phrases like "I *see* what you mean" and "I like/don't like the *look* of that". They talk louder and faster than other people, and they walk faster and with their head held up.

They don't want details, they want pictures. So show them brochures and talk to their imagination by painting a compelling future for them with your product.

Paint a bright picture – and put them in it.

When talking to Visual people, keep your energy high and use words like "picture", "show", "imagine", "perspective" and "see".

Visual people will buy a new car on how it looks – and how it will make them look. They want to get in and out quickly, make the purchase and move on. It is therefore vital to test close a Visual early and often.

To make an appointment with a Visual, say: *"How is Tuesday LOOKING for you? Shall we SEE each other at 10am or 11am?"*

Auditory people

Auditory people make purchasing decisions based on how something SOUNDS to them. They like to be given lots of information and to hear all the benefits before making a decision. They will usually buy for rational reasons.

They use phrases like: "I *hear* what you are saying" and "That *sounds* interesting."

They talk at a measured pace. And, yes, these are the people who can tend to drone on a bit if you let them.

Auditory people carry their heads level and their energy is set on "medium". When talking to them, keep your energy at a medium level as well and make sure you have lots of passion in your voice. Use words like "listen", "talk", "hear", "tune in" and "sounds like."

A phrase an Auditory person loves to hear is: *"Let's sit down and talk this through."*

To make an appointment with an Auditory, say: *"How does Tuesday SOUND for you? Shall we SAY 10am or 11am?"*

Kinesthetic people

Kinesthetic people make purchasing decisions based primarily on how they FEEL about you, and secondly how they FEEL about the product or service you are offering them.

Like Visuals, they will usually buy for emotional reasons and then later justify their decision to buy with rational reasons.

With Kinesthetics it is particularly important that you make them feel comfortable at all times, right from the moment you walk in.

They use phrases like: "That *feels* good" or "Something doesn't *feel* right" or "I am/am not *comfortable* with that".

They talk slowly and softly and they carry their heads down to be in touch with the rest of their body. They want to feel comfortable at all costs.

When talking to Kinesthetic people, keep your energy and volume low (but still remain enthusiastic and passionate) and use words like "feel", "comfortable", "exciting", "passionate" and "peace of mind".

Remember, you can still be energised and enthusiastic while remaining "low down and intimate". It is all in the voice, the eyes and the body language. Use your hands to gesticulate and your eyes to transmit your passion about what you are saying.

(In fact, use your hands for all VAKs: up and joyous for Visuals; cup your ears for Auditories; hold your heart for Kinesthetics.)

To make an appointment with a Kinesthetic, say: *"How do you FEEL about Tuesday? Would you be more COMFORTABLE with 10am or 11am?"*

* * *

How to determine which is which

The quickest and easiest way to determine if someone is Visual, Auditory or Kinesthetic when you are face-to-face with them is to ask a question that forces them to think back in their memory before answering.

The perfect question for this exercise is: *"When was the last time you bought something that you felt really happy with?"*

As they think about their answer, watch where their eyes go as they delve into their memory banks:

– Visuals' eyes will go up or defocus.

– Auditories' eyes will go to the side.

– Kinesthetics' eyes will go down.

The other way to determine if someone is Visual, Auditory or Kinesthetic is to listen to their buzz words and phrases and to watch the way they move.

– Visuals have high energy levels, hold their head up and talk and move fast. Their hands are usually waving about. And they say words and phrases like "I see" and "that looks good".

– Auditories have medium energy levels, hold their head level and talk and move at a measured pace. Their hands are usually by their side or in their pockets. And they say words like "sounds good" and "I hear you".

– Kinesthetics have low energy levels, hold their head down and talk and move slowly and intimately. Their hands are usually in touch with their own body or stroking their hair or clutching their knees. And they say words like "feel" and "comfortable".

Digital people

There is a fourth category that is usually found in extremely Auditory people and is useful to be able to recognise. Digital people love details. The more information they can get about a product or service, the happier they feel – and they won't usually make a decision without first having ALL the facts.

These people can be a pain because selling them takes so much effort. But they can be wooed with phrases like: *"Do you want to hear about some of the really amazing details that I know you are going to love?"*

Or: *"Let's talk about the really important details that I know you want to go through one by one".*

If you said this to a Visual or a Kinesthetic person, they would probably run a mile.

Step 5. Lead them

This is a refinement of Matching in Step 4 and is used (both on the phone and in person) when the customer is a down state.

Obviously, if they are feeling down and depressed it is important that you first match them to create rapport, but you don't want to leave them there. Otherwise you are now both feeling depressed!

So as soon as you have gained rapport, made them feel comfortable and have earned their trust, slowly start bringing them up by raising your energy levels.

People subconsciously like to stay in rapport, so they will usually follow you up just to stay in alignment with you.

You need to do this gradually, though. And if at any time you lose them, just go back down and deepen the rapport before bringing them slowly back up again.

The reason this is important is because people seldom make decisions – especially purchasing decisions – when they are down and depressed. So you need to lift their mood before you can hope to persuade them to buy, and buy now.

Step 6. Mirror them

Another great way to create rapport with a person on a subliminal level and make them like you – because you are "just like them" – is to mirror their body language. In other words, to copy the way they sit, stand and move.

If you do this subtly they won't notice what you are doing, but they will subconsciously feel a great surge of affinity with you.

Examples:

– If they are sitting back with their legs crossed in a certain way, do the same.

– If they are sitting forward steepling their hands at their chin, do the same.

– If they lean back and link their hands behind their head, do the same.

– Copy their gestures too, but do it subtly. If they swing their arms like they are holding an imaginary golf club, for example, do the same – but only once and never at the same time as them. You don't want to be obvious.

If you watch a couple who are very much in love sitting together, their physiologies will usually be almost identical... and they don't even know they are doing it.

Fine-tune this further by breathing the way they do, nodding your head exactly as they do, copying the muscular tensions they have – and not only will they like you, but amazingly you will also start to feel the same things they are, thus allowing you to truly grasp how they are feeling and what they are thinking.

Step 7. Matchers and Mismatchers

When it comes to social interactions, there are two types of people: Matchers and Mismatchers.

Matchers are people who subconsciously like to align with the person who is talking to them and agree with what they are saying (even if they don't.). They do this because they like harmony and they dislike conflict. It is therefore very easy to create rapport with a Matcher.

Mismatchers are people who like to be different and stand out from the crowd. When someone is talking to them, they automatically look for things in what that person is saying to disagree with.

We've all met people like this, haven't we?

To create rapport with a Mismatcher, never fight them or even disagree with them. Simply let them have their little "victories" and respond with phrases such as: *"Fair enough"* and *"Yes, you have a point"*.

* * *

So, I've got a question for you. Who do you think it would be easier to sell to: a Matcher, or a Mismatcher?

You might think it would be the Matcher. But actually these people can be very elusive because they tend not to telegraph their true feelings.

So while they are nodding away and agreeing with you and saying things like "Yes, I know exactly what you mean." and "That sounds great", they might actually be thinking to themselves: *"This person's a turkey! There's no way I'm EVER going to buy one of those."*

Mismatchers, on the other hand, telegraph their opinions much more readily and in doing so give you a clear idea of what it is they want. You can often sell a Mismatcher by telling them your product may not be for them. Believe it or not, some will say they want it just to avoid having to agree with you.

I'm sure you've heard of The Takeaway – when you show someone your most expensive product and run through all its amazing features, and then take it away from them, saying: *"This is probably too much for you, though. Let me show you something less expensive."*

The Takeaway works brilliantly with aspirers; ie, people who aspire to a better class of life. And it also works perfectly with Mismatchers.

To sell to a Matcher you need to beware of the trap of mistaking their agreement for enthusiasm.

These are the people who will align with you and get in great rapport with you right from the start, but then just at the point when you think you are doing great and start assuming the sale, they will suddenly say: *"Let me think about it."*

To avoid this, simply make sure that throughout your sales presentation you have created enough units of interest (which we will cover in Chapter 5 in a moment), and also enough units of conviction, (which we will cover in Chapter 7).

* * *

2. Find out their values

Now that you have established great rapport with your customer so that they like you, you next need to find out exactly what their core values are – at least as they relate to the product or service you are offering.

This is crucial so that you can meet their needs, and it is done with the cunning use of questions that are designed to get them to open up and reveal information to you that you can use to align with them.

What are 'values'?

Our values rule our life. Values are the labels we give to what causes us pain or pleasure.

Every decision we make is based on our hierarchy of values. It is therefore crucial to elicit someone's values if you want to influence them and build lasting rapport with them.

It is very simple to find out someone's values. Just ask them: *"What do value most in your business / relationship / job / life / car / mobile phone / office equipment?"*

Depending on their answer you can now tailor your sales presentation to match their values.

Note:

When asking an intimate question, such as someone's values, it is often a good idea to get their permission first – especially if you have only just met them for the first time.

Ask: *Do you mind if I ask you a question?"* and wait for them to give you their approval before asking: *"What do you value most in...?"*

If you already have good rapport you can assume their approval by saying: *"Do you mind if I ask what you value most in...?"*

Make sure that you write down or memorise their answers because in the next step on our "10-Step Ladder to Sales Success and Total World Domination" in Chapter 5 you will want to tailor the benefits of your product to suit what they value most.

For example, if their No 1 value is affordability, you will highlight the money-saving features. If it's reliability, you will of course emphasise this aspect. And so on.

* * *

To finish up this chapter on rapport-building, I want to quickly run through what I call my "Communication Check-List".

This is a list of 10 advanced communication skills that will turn you into a Master Communicator who is able to connect and make friends with anyone and everyone you talk to in any given situation. You are already familiar with most of them.

Communication Check-List

1. Give them a time frame up front so you know you have their attention.

2. Speak like them by matching their tone, speed, volume, pitch etc.

3. Use their "buzz phrases" and "buzz words".

4. Match their VAK, both on the phone and in person.

5. Mirror their body language.

6. Ask lots and lots of questions. This a) allows them to talk about themselves, which makes them happy, and b) gives you vital information on which to base your sales pitch to suit their specific needs and wants.

7. Beware using the word "but" because it negates what you just said ("I really like that, but..."). Try to use "and" instead. Remember: "and" builds bridges; "but" builds walls.

8. Always align with them. Never disagree, even when they are wrong. You can always use these cop-out phrases if you must: "Well, you have a point" and "Well, I can see/hear/feel that you are passionate about this."

9. Use laughter a lot, but not so much that you appear flippant. Everyone loves to have fun, and the more fun you can be, the more your clients will want to spend time with you.

10. Pay attention. Develop your Sensory Acuity so you know exactly how they are feeling all the time and you are able to respond and adjust your behaviour accordingly.

Write out this list and put it up above your desk. These 10 skills need to become second nature to you so you do all of them without even thinking about it.

Step 5:
Make them love it...

Grab their attention and fire up their desire

NOW that you have established rapport, and have hopefully put your customer in a great state, you want to anchor their great state to your product or service by beginning your presentation right away.

This step is all about making them interested in what you have to sell, and you do this by creating what Tony Robbins calls Units of Interest. Then, as soon as you feel you have built up enough Units of Interest, come straight out and ask them if they are ready to buy by using what we in the sales trade call a Test Close.

There are FIVE steps to creating a Unit of Interest:

1. Make a big claim

"This printer has the potential to totally transform your business."

2. Support your claim with a fact

"The reason I say that is because you will be able to create promotional materials far beyond what you are capable of doing now and radically increase your sales almost immediately."

3. State a compelling benefit for them

"What that means to you is a massive boost to your profit and a much more effective sales team."

4. State a more personal benefit

"And what that REALLY means to you is that you will have the freedom to grow your business in any way you want to."

5. Give evidence for all your statements

"This machine has already done this for countless customers of mine. In fact, if you like I'd be happy to put you in touch with a few of them so you can find out for yourself just what amazing results they are getting."

Exercise

Pull out a notebook and pen and create three Units of Interest for whatever product or service you are currently selling.

Make a big claim and a fact to back it up. Then write down two appealing benefits (the first financial and the second personal), and a compelling piece of evidence.

* * *

Test closes

As soon as you have created two or more Units of Interest with your customer, you want to start testing to see if they are ready to buy. Sometimes one Unit of Interest is all they need. Other times you might need to create several.

The way to see where they are at with regards to making a decision to buy is by using a Test Close.

<u>A Test Close goes like this:</u>

"So, in your opinion, if we can show you how much benefit you will get from installing these machines, would you be prepared to go ahead?"

(Note: The *"in your opinion..."* frame is a truly magical subliminal technique that can be used to take the "heat" out of a difficult or personal question. Subconsciously, you are making them feel that they are not giving you a definitive answer, merely their opinion of what they would say if they were to answer you. This makes it much easier for them to say "Yes".)

Test closes are a sales person's best friend. They always take the form of a question, and they always give the customer a choice of two alternatives.

<u>For example:</u>

"In your opinion, if you were to go ahead, would you want the car in the hard top or the brand new convertible model?"

Or:

"In your opinion, if you were to go ahead, would you want just one machine, or two or three to really ramp up your sales presentations?"

You should be test closing throughout your presentation because some buyers may be ready to buy right from the start and just need to be asked.

* * *

There are three types of Test Close:

1 The opening Test Close

This is the one we have just done. It is based on your Units of Interest and is done before you have even asked them what it is they really want.

2. The progressive Test Close

Once you know what they want, you can race ahead to assume the sale: *"So if I can show you how this machine can do all you want, and more, would you want it installed straight away? I think I might even be able to pull some strings and have it installed for you tomorrow?"*

3. The trade-off Test Close

The third type of test close is used to satisfy an objection: *"So in your opinion, if we can solve the issue of price, would you be thinking of just one machine or getting a discount on two or more?"*

Note the structure of this last question. Rather than asking: "Would you be willing to go ahead?" you are trying to up-sell them by asking if they would like more than one at a discount. You should always be looking for ways to up-sell, because you just never know. After all, if you don't ask, you don't get.

* * *

After you have given them one of these three Test Closes, if they are keen you can go straight to Chapter 8 and assume the sale.

If you get a negative response to a Test Close, the first and most important thing to do is stay in alignment with them by agreeing with them.

Tell them they are right to want to know more and then move on to the next step of your presentation – probing for their needs and wounds.

Say something like: "I totally understand. And rather than me going on about how amazing this machine is, wouldn't it be much better if YOU told ME exactly what you are looking for so that I can customise a solution that's perfect for you?"

Get their permission by waiting for a definite "Yes". Then say: *"Great, then let me ask you just a couple of quick questions."*

And move straight on to the next step...

Step 6:
Make them need it!

Dig deeper and stir up their emotions

THE purpose of this stage is to stir them up. You need to find out exactly what your customer wants and what they lack, and to make them fully associated to all the pain they are feeling from NOT having what they want right now, as well as all the pleasure they will experience when they get what they want – and more – from buying your product or service.

The magic of leverage

To change someone's mind, their beliefs, or their behaviour patterns you need to get leverage on them.

In other words, it's not enough to simply show or tell someone about pain and pleasure. You also need to get them to fully associate enough pain to their present thought patterns, beliefs and actions and enough pleasure to a new course of action so that they will change their behaviour.

No one will ever change until they have enough leverage to change. And in this case we want our customer to change their mind and buy our product or service the next time we use a Test Close.

[*Important warning:* Before we go any further, I want to reiterate what I said at the start of this book: that although the subliminal skills you are learning in this book are astonishingly powerful for influencing other people to do what you want them to do, they will not work if you try to use them without integrity. Sure, you might be able to persuade one or two people to buy something they don't really want or need, but very quickly you will pay a heavy price for your dishonesty in terms of lost income, ill health and possibly worse. I don't mean to scare you, it's just the truth.]

* * *

How to get leverage

The best way to get leverage on someone quickly is to ask effective questions combined with VAK.

Questions are crucial. Sales guru Tom Hopkins once said: "When YOU say it, they can doubt you. When THEY say it, it's the truth."

Examples of leverage questions:

— "What's the BEST THING about the widget you are using now? How would you FEEL if you could do that much cheaper?" (Pleasure)

— "What's the WORST THING about the widget you have now? And how does that make you FEEL?" (Pain)

— "What's the one thing you wish your widget could do better? I bet you'd LOVE to be able to do (blank). Isn't that right? How would you FEEL if you could do that?" (Pleasure)

— "What is it costing you right now in lost sales and lost business because your widget can't (blank)? How does that make you FEEL?" (Pain)

— "How many customers do you think you are not winning at the moment by not being able to do this?" (Pain)

— "Even worse, how many of your customers could you LOSE when they find out that they can get this from one of your competitors much cheaper than what you can offer now? What would that COST YOU?" (Pain)

— "How much money would you MAKE if you could do (blank)?" (Pleasure)

— "How much money would you SAVE if you could do (blank)?" (Pleasure)

— "What will it cost you if you CAN'T do (blank)?" (Pain)

— "What could you do with the $20,000 a year you'll save by installing this new widget? How would that make you FEEL?" (Pleasure)

Remember to use their VAK to make them fully associate to the pain and pleasure.

Deep down we are all Kinesthetic, so although you will want to phrase your questions according to their VAK programming, you will also want to tack on to the end of each question the more intense question: *"How does (or would) that make you FEEL?"*

Visual:

"How would it look if...? How would that make you feel?"

"Imagine if you could... How would that make you feel?"

"Can you picture yourself telling your boss that you have just saved the company $20,000? How would that make you feel?"

Auditory:

"How does it sound to be able to save $20,000?" And how would that make you feel?"

"What would your boss say to you if you could save him $20,000? And how would that make you feel?"

Kinesthetic

"How does it feel?"

"How would you feel?"

"Imagine how you would feel if..."

* * *

Now that you have your customer fully associated to all the PAIN they are feeling because of what their widget is unable to do, and all the PLEASURE they will get as a result of buying yours, it's time to go to Step 7 and get them to convince themselves that they must have what you are selling – and they must have it NOW.

PART THREE:

COMPEL

Step 7:
Hook 'em...

Create conviction and remove all doubt

THIS is the heart of your presentation when you take the customer's responses to your emotion-stirring questions from Step 6 in the previous chapter and answer them one by one by creating Units of Conviction for each of them.

Units of Conviction are exactly the same as the Units of Interest that we created in Chapter 5, except that they have a Test Close attached to the end of them.

<u>Example:</u>

"You stated that the two most important aspects of your printing requirements are to be able to produce far more impressive sales presentation materials than you can now, but for an absolute minimum extra cost."

Then show them how your machine can do just that with a six-step Unit of Conviction:

1. Make a big claim

"The T1000 here is the perfect machine for you because it will give you everything you have just told me you need, while keeping the cost to an absolute minimum."

2. Support it with a fact

"The reason I say that is because the T1000 is on special at the moment at just $16,000, for which you will get all the features you want and more."

3. State a benefit for them

"What that means for you is that you will be able to run rings around your competitors, which as you said is one of the best ways to boost your sales."

4. State a more personal benefit

"And what that REALLY means for you is that your earnings will skyrocket, which is going to make your boss very happy with you. And we won't even TALK about the juicy big bonus that you're going to get."

5. Give evidence for these claims

"I have one client of mine who doubled her sales within six months of installing one of these machines. She was so thrilled she even sent me a case of wine for Christmas to say thank you."

6. Test close (with Double Bind)

"So, in your opinion, do you want to go ahead with the T1000, or would you like to consider one of the bigger models like the T2000 that give you more bang for your buck but may be more than you need right now?"

If they agree you can assume the sale and go straight to Step 8.

However, if they are still wavering simply create more Units of Conviction by tackling another of the hurts or wants you established in the previous step.

Exercise

Pull out a notebook and pen and create three Units of Conviction for whatever product or service you are currently selling.

Make a big claim and a fact to support it. Then write down two appealing benefits (the first financial and the second personal), back them up with a compelling piece of evidence and finish with an effective Test Close.

* * *

Tipping the balance

Everyone has a little see-saw in their mind when thinking about buying something. On one side of the see-saw are their Emotional Reasons to Buy (*"I will be so much happier when I have it"*) and their Rational Excuses to Buy (*"This offer won't last long, so I should get in while I can."*). Then on the other side are all their Reasons to Avoid Buying (*"It's too expensive"* or *"I don't really need it right now – I can get one next year when I have more money"*.)

The see-saw looks like this:

People like to think that they buy for purely logical reasons, but the truth is most people buy for emotional reasons and then justify the purchase to themselves – and others – with logical reasons.

Think of someone who buys a new outfit in the sales. They know they can't afford it (RAB), but they also know they will look great in it which will give them tonnes of pleasure (ERB). So they buy the outfit and then justify it to themselves – and their partner – with: "It was 20 per cent off." (REB).

This is just as true in business. The process of creating Units of Conviction is to pile up the ERB and REB on one side and remove the RAB from the other side so the see-saw topples and they buy now, not later.

* * *

Use questions to discover where they are at on their see-saw:

Example 1

— *"On a scale of 1 to 100, 100 being you are certain you want to go ahead, where would you say you are right now?"*

— *"What would I have to do to take you to 100 right now?"*

Example 2

— *"Is this something you are committed to doing now, providing you are happy with the price?"*

— *"Then isn't the real question: how do we make this happen right now?"*

Get a "yes"... and then drop the price.

Note about price:

Always try to give them a higher price up front in your presentation so that at this point you can drop it down to enroll them.

ॐ

Step 8:
Book 'em...

Assume the sale and do the paperwork

THE see-saw is now firmly tipped in your favour, so without further ado you can assume the sale and move straight on to the paperwork.

At this point it is vital that you maintain your enthusiasm at Level 10 or above. You need to make them as enthusiastic as possible about the prospect of owning your product because they are now getting close to the point of no return.

No matter how much they may want it, when someone is close to making a big purchase their brain sets off all sorts of doubts and their heads fill up with thoughts such as:

"Yes, but do I really NEED it?"
"Can I really AFFORD it?"
"Do I need it NOW, or should I wait?"

You need to drown out those voices while you get out the paperwork. In fact, keep it up even after they sign so that you can get great referrals from them and prevent the dreaded "buyer's remorse".

Three ways to maintain enthusiasm:

1. Be so infectiously enthusiastic that they feel it too:

– *"Excellent, I am so HAPPY for you."*

– *"You are going to LOVE having this machine."*

– *"Your sales team are going to think you're a total HERO when it makes their jobs so much easier."*

– *"Imagine how they will thank you when their commissions go THROUGH THE ROOF."*

2. Repeatedly state all the benefits, and bring in new ones you have held back deliberately for this phase to get them over the line:

– *"Something AMAZING about this machine that I forgot to tell you is that it also makes coffee, mows the lawn and does the washing-up."*

3. Paint a compelling future for them with your product:

– *"I am so excited for you. You are getting this at EXACTLY THE RIGHT TIME because you will be able to take full advantage of all those customers out there who have come through the economic slowdown and are now unbattoning the hatches and looking to re-stock their inventories."*

The moment of truth

Be aware that this is the point of no return, so no matter how enthusiastic you are and how much pleasure they are feeling, if there are any lingering objections in the customer's mind they will come up now.

If there are no objections, move straight to Step 10.

If an objection does come up, don't panic – simply move elegantly and seamlessly on to Step 9...

Step 9:
And cook 'em!

Turn their objections into commitments

MANY sales people dread objections, but all top sales professionals love them because they give us an opportunity to perform some truly magical sales alchemy by turning a customer's doubts into certainty.

When a customer tells you an objection, they are revealing what is really going on in their minds. This gives you an opportunity to satisfy their true desires, remove any lingering doubts and seal the deal.

Up until now your customer could have dismissed you with an *"I'm not interested"*. But you have created interest and conviction, and all that now stands in your way are their objections.

By giving you their objections, they are telling you they are keen to buy... providing their objections can be answered to their satisfaction.

This is fantastic news!

If they weren't keen, they would just say: *"No thank you."* But they aren't saying that. They are saying: *"It's too expensive."* Or: *"It's great, but I'm not sure I really need it."* Or perhaps the familiar: *"I'll think about it."*

* * *

There are 10 steps to turning an objection into a commitment. So let's run through them in turn, using as an example the most common objection of them all: *"It's too expensive."*

1. Ignore it

At the first mention of their objection just carry right on with the paperwork.

The human brain is hard-wired to reject things, rather than accept them, as a kind of knee-jerk reaction. For example, if you ask someone at dinner if they would like some more desert, they will almost always say: *"No thank you."* Press them, and they will probably come back with: *"Oh, all right then – yes please."*

The same is true here. Many people object subconsciously and they don't really mean it. So always ignore the first objection and carry on enthusiastically with the paperwork.

You'd be surprised how often they aren't really worried at all.

2. Hear them out

If they do repeat the objection, stop what you are doing and listen intently – using your eyes, your ears and your whole body – until they are finished.

At this point your energy needs to convey that you are concerned for their sake rather than for yours.

What do I mean by that? Well, think back to the very beginning of the book when I asked you to come from the frame of mind of someone who is giving the customer something that will be of great value to them – rather than someone who is hoping to make a sale in order to meet your monthly target.

So the look on your face – and the energy in your body – must be one of genuine concern that their objection is going to deny them what they really want. You are aligning with them to defeat the objection.

When they have repeated their objection, wait for a second to make sure they are finished, then...

3. Feed it back exactly

Say: *"It's too expensive?"*

Always repeat the words exactly as they said them, phrased as a question. Then shut up and wait for them to answer the question.

Make sure that your tone and expression display concern for them rather than irritation or disagreement.

You'll be amazed at how many people fill the silence by answering their own objection for you with something like: *"Well, I suppose it's not really that expensive."*

4. Question it

If they persist in telling you that they still think it is "too expensive", stay in rapport by nodding your head as though you understand what they are saying, but do NOT say that you agree with them.

Instead, look concerned and say these words exactly as they are written:

"I know you have a reason for saying that. Do you mind if I ask what it is?"

(Note: Don't say "good reason". You don't want to reinforce what they believe.)

5. Make it a final objection

After they have given you their reason for saying it is "too expensive", stay in alignment with them and say:

"So, is that your only concern? By that I mean, if WE (not "I") *can solve that, in your opinion would you want to go ahead?"*

(Note: As before, the "in your opinion" frame takes the sting out of the question.)

– If they say "Yes", go on to Step 6.

– If they say "No", go back to Step 3 and feed it back exactly with *"No?"* to find out what this new objection is.

In this way, get all their objections clearly stated and get them to agree that these are their final objections before going on to Step 6.

In the case of more than one objection, write them all down on a piece of paper in front of them and then handle them one at a time by going through these next five steps for each of them.

6. Align with them to defeat the objection
– "I totally agree with you, AND... (not "but")..."
– "Many people have told me that, AND..."

7. Turn it into a question
"...and that brings up a question, doesn't it? Isn't the question whether in spite of the cost, isn't it possible that you would actually get much more benefit than what you are investing?

"Isn't the real question not what it costs, but what it is WORTH to you?"

8. Answer the question
Now you can answer the question by showing them what great value your product is.

There are SIX different ways to do this, and you can remember them with this cute mnemonic: "QT N BED"

1. **Q**uestion it

"Having seen all the things this machine can do, do you mind if I ask you WHY you think it is expensive?"

2. **T**urn it around

"That's exactly why this is the BEST option for you. You have already told me that you have a great sales team and that they deserve the best presentation materials because you know they will be able to use them to make more sales. So this actually is the perfect machine for you. A lesser company with less-able sales professionals might make do with a cheaper machine – but then their revenue will be far less too."

3. **N**egate it

"Isn't the real question what would it cost you if you DONT buy it – in terms of lost sales and a less-professional corporate image in the marketplace, which I'm sure you'd agree is more competitive than ever?"

4. **B**reak it down

"Yes, it appears expensive on the surface, but it is actually a cheap investment when you add up the extra revenue it will earn you in a year. Over 12 months, it works out at just $XX a week, which I'm betting is less than you spend on coffee and stationery (or transport costs, or whatever is appropriate for your customer), which don't contribute directly to your bottom line like this machine does."

5. Explain it

"Yes, it is more expensive than the one you have now, you are absolutely right. Almost all my happiest customers said the same thing to me at first. But I was able to show them all the extra benefits they are now enjoying that made it actually MUCH BETTER VALUE than the machines they were using before. So let's do what I did with them and go through all the features that make it such good value for money. Would that be OK?"

6. Deny it

"So, as you can see, for what you are getting and for how much money it will make you, it isn't really expensive at all."

9. Tie them down

I don't mean literally tie them down... although you can if they're into it, I suppose. After all, I did say sales was supposed to be fun!

No, I mean ask them this question: *"So that solves that, doesn't it?"*

10. If 'No' go back to Step 3

If they say "No", go back to Step 3 and feed it back exactly with *"No?"*

If they say "Yes", do the paperwork and go to the final step in the next chapter.

* * *

How to handle "I'll think about it"

We've all heard this one a million times, haven't we? *"I'll think about it"* and *"I'll get back to you"* are a customer's default cop-out phrases. But what are they actually saying to you when they use them?

The truth is they are objecting to something, or else they would be buying. This simply means that you have not created enough Units of Interest and Units of Conviction earlier in your presentation. So you need to find out what their objection is, and you do this with (yes, you guessed it!)... a question.

"I completely understand. Let's think this out together. What about XYZ is not absolutely perfect for you yet?"

– If they come back with their real objection, go back to Step 3 and feed it back exactly. Then run through the steps as before to solve it.

– If they persist with: "Oh no, it's great. I just want to think it over", you now run the risk of being pushy if you go in too hard. So instead you say:

"I can see/hear/feel (depending on their VAK) *that you're not convinced. Do you mind if I ask you, on a scale of one to five, if one is not at all interested and five is "I absolutely must have this now", in your opinion where are you right now?"*

After they give you a number, say:

"That's great. You know, I am so passionate about how perfect this is for you – and I have grown to like you so much that

I really don't want you to miss out. So in your opinion, what would I have to do right now to take you all the way up to a five?"

Note: Of course, the best way to handle "I'll think about it" is to see it coming before they say it. That way you can pre-empt their objection by bringing it up yourself with: *"I see that you're not YET completely sure. What have I missed out?"*

* * *

How to handle "I don't know"

In sales, customers often say "I don't know" in response to a question, either because they haven't bothered to think about it properly or because they are reluctant to reveal what they are really thinking.

A powerful way to get them to give you a proper answer to your question is to first agree with them, then ask a supposition question that appears to be far less demanding:

"I know you don't know... but just imagine for a moment that you DID know... what do you think it COULD be?"

This can also work for "I don't want to":

"I understand you don't want to now... but if you WERE to, imagine how wonderful you COULD feel."

ॐ

PART FOUR:

CELEBRATE

Step 10:
Moonwalk outta there!

Get referrals and leave them hap-hap-happy

CONGRATULATIONS! Your job is done. You have made the sale, got the signature... and your big, fat, juicy commission is on the way.

But don't start looking at those Ferrari brochures just yet. There is one crucial step left.

Before you put the contract in your pocket or your bag and **Moonwalk backwards out of their office** in celebration you want to make sure that your customer is feeling absolutely fantastic about having invested their hard-earned cash in your product or service.

There are three reasons for this:

1. You don't want them to develop buyer's remorse after you have gone and ask for their money back during the "cooling-off" period.

2. You want to get some great referrals off them. Remember, having a referral is of enormous value to you when it comes to calling your next prospects.

3. Plus you want to make sure all your customers are happy little customers who will keep their business with you. Never forget the Marketing Manager's mantra: *"It is far easier to keep a customer than make a new one."*

* * *

There are four steps involved in making them happy and getting great referrals:

1. Congratulate them

"Congratulations. You have made a fantastic choice. I know you are going to be so happy with this printer."

2. Paint a bright picture of the future and put them in it

Use VAK to maximise the pleasure for them, based on whether they are visual, auditory or kinesthetic:

— *"Imagine the look on your boss's face when he sees next month's sales figures."*

— *"Imagine what your boss is going to say when you tell him about next month's sales figures."*

— *"Imagine how incredible you are going to feel when you give your boss next month's sales figures."*

3. Let them know they have a friend

Reassure them that you will be around for a very long time. Tell them that if there are any setting-up niggles, you or a technician will be right round to iron them all out straight away.

Also, if they have any questions, no matter how small, you are available on your mobile at any time.

4. Get your referrals

This is a great time to invoke the Law of Reciprocation because you are going to ask them for something – and they will be far more likely to give it to you if you give them something first. It doesn't have to be anything big (remember the coffee from Chapter 3).

So if you are selling advertising space in a print publication, you could say:

"Gosh, I've just realised... I may be able to get you a right-hand page."

Or advertising on TV:

"I've just realised... I may be able to get you a free promotional slot during the prime-time breakfast show."

Or if it's a product:

"I've just realised... I may be able to throw in a couple of free toner cartridges / a month's free calls / a free tank of petrol etc."

Tell them you'll have to check with head office whether it's OK, but you're sure it will be. Then move straight on to ask for what you want.

This is an excellent script for getting referrals:

"Can I just ask you for something in return? It may be too soon for you to be able to do this now, but once the machine is up and running and you are totally happy with it, would it be possible for you to give me the names of some of your friends or family members who are in business who you feel might also benefit from a machine like this?

"I promise to conduct myself with them in exactly the same honest and professional manner as I have with you, and to respect them exactly as I have respected you. Would that be ok with you?"

You are going to be checking back with them anyway – a good salesperson always follows up to make sure they are happy, especially if it is a big-ticket item – so you can get your referrals then.

But you really want some referrals NOW. Plus, you are dangling a free gift in front of them, so push a little by getting out your notebook and saying:

"In fact, it might be fantastic if I could get some brochures off to a couple of them right away. Who, right off the top of your head, do you think would benefit the most?"

Write it all down and thank them profusely.

Say goodbye.

And NOW – finally – you have arrived at the best part when you get to...

MOONWALK OUTTA THERE!

No, not THAT kind of Moonwalk...

THIS KIND!

But wait... there's more!
10 bonus sales skills

Yep, these little gems are completely free of charge

1. State questions in the positive

Always try to phrase your questions to get the response you want.

Don't steer the other person to say no to you by making your questions negative in the misguided belief that you are being polite. You want to steer them towards agreeing with you and saying yes.

Notice the difference between saying:
- *"I don't suppose you could...?"*
- *"I don't suppose you have time to...?"*

And saying:
- *"Can you please...?"*
- *"Do you have time to do this quickly now please?"*

* * *

2. Use embedded commands

Embedded commands are hidden words that are designed to persuade someone to do what you want them to do. They work on a person's subconscious mind, which hears them as a call to action.

In these two examples the embedded commands are in capital letters and are used to upsell a customer:

– *"You probably haven't thought to BUY FIVE WIDGETS INSTEAD OF TWO, but if that is what you really want it might be worth considering the discounts available and the extra benefits they would give you."*

– *"I won't ask you to BUY FIVE WIDGETS, but if that is what you want to consider I would be happy to outline the discounts you would get."*

* * *

3. Use Transformational Vocabulary

The words you use determine how you feel – and, in a sales context, how your customer feels as well. So try to use words that make you – and them – feel fantastic:

- "Excellent" instead of "good".
- "Wonderful" instead of "all right".
- "Ecstatic" instead of "happy".
- "Passionate" instead of "keen".
- "A bit put out" instead of "angry".

– "A challenge" instead of "a problem".

– "An opportunity" instead of "an obstacle".

* * *

4. Anchors wahey!

An anchor is a creative association between a specific stimulus and a specific emotional state. Smells, for example, or certain songs can be powerful anchors.

We are all anchoring and being anchored all the time, whether we know it or not, so it pays to be aware of how they operate in both your business life and your personal relationships.

Negative anchors are the cause of most relationship breakdowns. When we spend a lot of time with someone, negative anchors get set up without us even realising that it is happening.

If we have a fight and see their face, or come home from work feeling grumpy and see their face, or watch our favourite sports team lose on TV and then see their face, we are subconsciously associating their face to the negativity we are feeling.

Pretty soon we might be feeling great but then we see their face and… whammo! All of a sudden we feel bad and we don't even know why. But we figure it must have something to do with them.

To avoid this trap, simply spend as much time as you can in your relationship setting up positive anchors by laughing and playing together whenever possible.

In business, the same dynamic applies...

You can use anchors with your customers to great effect. When they are laughing and feeling good, do something specific to anchor them to that state. The best anchor is a combination of a movement and a sound.

Examples might include reaching out to touch them on the shoulder and saying "That's right!", or clicking your fingers and saying "Excellent!".

The more times you can do this, the stronger the anchor will be. Always do the EXACT same thing and do it at the PEAK of their positive emotional state.

The purpose is so that later, perhaps when they are feeling a little nervous about signing the paperwork, you can fire off the anchor to help them to feel great.

Also, whenever they are laughing or feeling in peak state, make sure that you point to your product or talk about it so they anchor a connection between feeling great and your product.

Equally, when they are not feeling great, don't talk about your product or show it to them. Use a pattern interrupt (see No. 5 below), make them feel great again and THEN anchor them to your product.

Self-anchoring

Another kind of anchoring is called self-anchoring. This involves pointing at yourself when you are saying something like: *"I can tell what you really need is a man/woman who is totally honest and reliable and on your side."*

You can also point to your product and say*: "What you need is a machine that can do X, Y and Z seamlessly without breaking down and at a fraction of the price you might think it would cost."*

Anchoring yourself and your product are powerful subliminal tools that you can use to build up a positive attitude in your customer. If you do it subtly, they won't notice what you are doing, but their subconscious mind will link what you are saying to you and your product.

* * *

5. Interrupt their pattern

Do you know how some people just get stuck on a negative track and go on and on about something negative, like a broken record?

If your customer starts doing this during your presentation, you can't risk merely interrupting them without running the risk of destroying your carefully constructed rapport. Instead, what you want to do is shock them out of their "stuck state" by doing or saying something unexpected.

You need to prepare a number of different pattern interrupts that you can do well and that work. Trial and error is the best way for this. Once you find two or three that work for you and that you are comfortable doing, stick with them.

The more rapport you have, the more outrageous – and therefore the more effective – the pattern interrupts can be.

And if you can get them to move as well, it's even better because it will change their energy radically.

Here are three that I have used with great effect:

1. Make a sudden movement

If they are droning on and on, you can interrupt their pattern by shifting in your chair and suddenly saying *"Ouch!"* quite loudly as you grab your arm or your leg.

Make sure they have stopped talking and then say: *"I am so sorry. It's OK, just a cramp I think."*

Then repeat your apology by saying: *"I'm so sorry, what were you saying?"*

But don't let them answer and get back into their negative rant. Instead, continue straight on by answering your own question like this:

"Oh, that's right, you were saying how tough the economy is and how everyone in your industry is doing it tough at the moment."

Then ask a question that steers them where you want them to go so they are talking more positively again:

"That is a really interesting point and you make it very well. And, in fact, it actually brings up a question, doesn't it? Isn't the question: How can we quickly and cheaply steal a march on our competitors while they are struggling, so we can carve out a bigger share of the market while their guard is down?"

2. Make them move

As they are droning on, and while you continue to listen to them intently so as not to appear rude, spread out some brochures on the desk facing you and get them to stand up and come around to your side of the desk to look at them. You then continue with your presentation.

3. Say something unexpected

While they are speaking, wait for a gap and say: *"Hmmm… yes… well, that's the trouble with keeping geese!"*

They will almost certainly stop and say: *"WHAT??"*

You must then tailor your response depending on the nature of their rant.

1. If they were going on and on about how bad the economy is, you can say: *"A friend of mine farms geese – you know for their down – and he says people just aren't buying luxury*

pillows at the moment. He has had to cut all his office costs down to the bone, just like you. Which is why this budget-priced widget is absolutely perfect for you right at this moment."

2. If they were saying how competitive the market is and they are losing ground to their competitors and don't have any money to spend, you say this:

"A friend of mine in the UK farms geese – you know for their down – and he says that so many people have come into the industry of late that his profit margins have halved and he never has any money to invest in new equipment.

"I told him the quality of his product was entirely dependent on the quality of his equipment and he should take out a loan and upgrade his machinery and blow his competitors out of the water by offering his customers a much better product than the others can.

"That's exactly what he did and he is now raking it in. And it's exactly what you could do too. Right now, you can buy the best widget on the market (point to your brochure as you say this to anchor your product to what you are saying) *and blow all your competitors away. Just like my friend did."*

Have fun creating your own pattern interrupts. Just please be aware that these examples are ones that work for me. You must make sure that yours are congruent with your personality and your presentation style.

* * *

6. Framing

You need to become excellent at framing conversations with people so you can control what they focus on as the two of you are talking.

There are THREE types of framing:

1. Pre-framing

You want to handle objections before they even arise using a pre-frame to get your customer to focus on the positive aspects of something you know they would otherwise have regarded as a negative.

This is done before the sales process even starts. For example, if you are selling someone a house which is out of town and you know they wanted to live close to their work, start by saying you have found this idyllic home in the most beautiful setting with a massive garden for your children to play in that is safe and right near a river where you can teach them to fish on weekends and you can even get a boat with all the money you will save.

They are now thinking of all great things that will make them happy rather than the long commute.

You then say: *"It is a little further out than you had thought about, but in all honesty I just have to show it to you because I know you are going to agree with me that a mere half an hour extra each day so you can live in an absolute paradise is going to be so worth it."*

A product pre-frame could go like this:

Let's say you know your customer likes your top-of-the-range widget but thinks it's too expensive. You need to pre-frame them into thinking that it is excellent value for money. So you arrive at your appointment a little flustered and say:

"Gosh, I'm so sorry – I had to run here to make it on time because our regional manager called us into an emergency sales meeting to tell us that because we've been selling so many T1000s they are putting up the price.

"Apparently, they have been so popular they reckon they must be underpriced. Anyway, it doesn't matter because you were probably going to go for one of the cheaper models without all those extra features.

"So anyway, how have you been? I hope your day hasn't been as crazy as mine."

2. Re-framing

Use questions to re-frame someone's viewpoint about your product during the sales process – in other words, to change the way they view your product.

Again, let's take the most common concern of "it's too expensive". You need to force them to re-evaluate their opinion with:

"Did you take your family away on holiday this year? Where did you take them? That sounds fantastic. I know this is really

cheeky and I normally wouldn't ask, but do you mind telling me how much you paid for it including travel and meal expenses and accommodation and everything?"

Or:

"In your opinion, how much do you think it would cost you if you don't buy this machine and your competitors do? How many customers do you think their sales teams will be able to steal away from you with their vastly superior presentation materials? I'm not saying it would happen, of course, but it could. Had you thought of it that way?"

3. De-framing

When all else fails, you can use de-framing to destroy someone's frame:

"Five years ago this widget would have cost three times as much, but because of the latest manufacturing technologies developed by XYZ ahead of their more cumbersome rivals like ABC – who aren't as able as we are to upgrade our product lines as quickly – this is actually incredibly good value."

Perhaps the most effective way of de-framing someone is to shock them into focusing on something completely different. For example, if they are focusing on what's wrong with your product, interrupt them suddenly by saying:

"I was just wondering as you were speaking... when are you next going on holiday? Do you mind if I ask?"

They will have to completely refocus in order to answer the question.

Let's say they tell you that they have no plans for a holiday. This is what you say to them:

"Excellent. That means you'll be here for a while. What I suggest we do is install one of these widgets for you for a week or so on a trial basis at no charge so that you can get a real feeling for all its amazing features.

"Between you and me, my boss hates it when I do this. But in your case I am so confident that you will end up wanting to keep it that I know I'll be able to placate him.

"And obviously, if you're not absolutely in love with it I will take it away with no questions asked and at absolutely no cost or inconvenience to you."

If they ARE going on holiday, say:

"Excellent. That means when you come back you'll be much more relaxed and I'll be able to sell you easily." (Laugh and align with them).

"No seriously, what I suggest we do is when you get back we install one of these widgets for you... etc."

* * *

7. Time management

Always try to manage the time in front of your customer according to the 80/20 rule. This rule states that they should be talking (and you listening intently) for 80 per cent of the time, and you should be talking for only 20 per cent of the time.

As they are communicating their feelings and emotions to you, they are subconsciously investing more and more in you, thereby increasing your value to them. Plus, the more they talk, the more information you can discover about them – which you can use to help you tailor your presentation to satisfy their wants and needs.

* * *

8. The Precision Model

You can use this five-pronged model to solve problems and disagreements quickly and easily when your customer is generalising. It is designed to cut through their generalisations and discover the specifics of what they are really thinking and feeling.

1. Universals: "All, every time, never"

Feed their generalisation back exactly as they said it: "All?" "Every time?" "Never?"

Examples

"People always let me down." ("Always?")
"All sales people are bastards." ("All of them?")
"Every time I see him he's angry." ("Every time?")

2. "Should, shouldn't, must, can't"

Use: "What would happen if?" and "What causes or prevents?" to get them to refocus.

<u>Examples</u>

"I can't do that." ("What's preventing you?")

"I shouldn't buy this now." ("What would happen if you did?")

3. Verbs

Ask them: "How specifically?"

<u>Examples</u>

"Sales people lie." ("How specifically?")

"Advertising doesn't work." ("How specifically?")

"Printers never work properly." ("How specifically?")

4. Nouns

Ask them: "Who or what specifically?"

<u>Examples</u>

"Business is absolutely terrible at the moment." ("In what way specifically?")

"We're having lots of problems." ("What specifically?")

"Our competitors are killing us." ("Who specifically?")

5. "Too much, too many, too expensive"

Ask them: "Compared to what?"

<u>Examples</u>

"It costs too much." ("Compared to what?")

"It takes too long." ("Compared to what?")

* * *

9. The SIX laws of unconscious persuasion

1. The Law of Reciprocation

When you give something to another person they automatically feel as though they have to give you something back.

You have felt this, haven't you, when someone gives you a gift at Christmas and you haven't bought them anything. Your focus as you open their present is not on their gift, but rather you are frantically thinking what you might have in the house that you could quickly wrap up and give them in return.

This law can be very powerful in sales. A simple gift like the cup of coffee in our example in Chapter 3 can generate in them a desire to give you the contract.

2. The Because frame

The word "because" has a magical effect on the human brain because people accept something much more readily if they are given a reason, even if it isn't really a real reason at all.

<u>Examples</u>

"I wonder if you could help me out... BECAUSE I need some help?"

"I'm sorry, but can I just jump the queue... BECAUSE I need to do this now?"

In both cases, you haven't actually given them a reason – but they will feel as though you have and therefore will be much more likely to agree. Of course, if you can give them a genuine reason, even better.

3. The Double Bind

The human mind is at its most comfortable when it feels it has a choice between two alternatives. If you just tell it what to do, it will resist. If you give it too many options, it will get confused. But if you give it two choices it will feel comfortable that it is both in control and getting what it wants.

The Double Bind plays on this by giving someone two choices, both of which are what you want them to do. If you merely ask someone to do something – a business person to make an appointment with you, or a customer to buy what you are selling – they have two choices: they can either agree to do it, or they can refuse to do it.

With the Double Bind, however, you give them two choices that both result in them making the appointment or buying your product or service. That way their subconscious mind never stops to think that it actually has a third choice… namely to say no.

Examples

— *"When would you prefer to see me: tomorrow at 10.30, or on Thursday at four?"*

— *"Which car would you prefer: the hard top, or the new convertible model?"*

In both these examples, it doesn't matter which option they choose because you will get the outcome you desire, while they will be happy because they feel they made a deliberate choice.

4. Social Proof

People like to feel that what they are doing or buying is in line with what the "smart people" are doing. They think: *"Well, if everyone's doing it, I should do it too."*

If you can, use examples of people they might admire who are already doing what you want them to do, or have already bought what you want them to buy.

"Microsoft just installed this machine, and Richard Branson owns two of them."

5. Commitment and consistency

Consistency is a value that is highly prized in our society. We tend to think good of people who are reliable and consistent, and we tend to look down on people who are flighty and unreliable.

You can use this to your advantage in sales by trying to get your customer to say "yes" as many times as possible throughout your presentation. Then, when it comes time for them to decide whether to buy your product or service, they will be reluctant to break with consistency by saying "no" to you.

The best way to do this is to tack "do you agree?" and "does that make sense?" on to the end of your sentences during your presentation.

If you can get your customer to say "yes" to you 50 times, when you then come to the point of asking them to buy, they are much less likely to break with consistency and say "no".

6. The Law of Contrast

Suppose a man enters a men's store and says he wants to buy a suit and a shirt. If you were the salesperson, which would you sell him first to make him likely to spend the most money?

You would sell him the suit first, because when it comes to look at shirts, even expensive ones, their prices will not be as high by comparison. He might baulk at the idea of spending $150 on a shirt, but if he has just bought a $800 suit, a $150 shirt doesn't seem excessive.

The same applies to the accessories (tie, shoes and belt) to go with his new suit and shirt.

Real estate agents have been known to use "set-up" properties. They keep a house or two on their lists at inflated prices. These houses are not intended to be sold but rather to be shown to prospects so that the genuine properties in the company's inventory benefit from having much lower prices by comparison.

To quote one estate agent: *"The house I have in mind for them looks great after they've first looked at a couple of similarly priced dumps."*

* * *

10. Handling difficult people

Finally, I want to wrap up this powerful little sales book by giving you some great tips on how to handle difficult people, whether they are customers or gatekeepers or colleagues at your work.

You will also find this information extremely beneficial in your personal life.

Understanding control dramas

In his best-selling books *The Celestine Prophecy* and *The Celestine Vision*, James Redfield explains how human beings compete for each other's energy as a result of a deep-seated subconscious existential insecurity. In other words, people often choose to make themselves feel better by making others focus on them – literally, by stealing their energy.

They do this by running what Redfield calls a Control Drama, which is basically a subconscious (and occasionally conscious in desperate people) behaviour pattern that is designed to gain control over others.

You will frequently find people playing Control Dramas in office environments, where insecure people feel they need to try to steal other people's energy and gain power over their perceived rivals.

There are four types of people who run these Control Dramas. Two of them are aggressive, and two of them are passive:

Aggressive:
The "Intimidator"
The "Interrogator"

Passive:
The "Aloof"
The "Poor Me"

The Intimidator
The strategy of the Intimidator is to win our attention, and thus our energy, by making us feel threatened – so we focus on them.

These are usually very angry people, and every office has them. If we cower or shrink back, they feel a little victory inside and receive the boost of energy they crave.

The Interrogator

Not quite as openly aggressive as Intimidators, Interrogators like to make themselves feel better by criticising us and asking us lots of questions to make us doubt ourselves. They get their victories – and their energy boost – when they make us buy into their view of the world.

The Aloof

Aloof people hang back and share very little information about themselves – the intention being, of course, that this forces others to pry further and thus focus on them.

They get their energy boost when we reach out to them or try to find out more about them.

The Poor Me

The most passive of the four Control Dramas, these are the "woe is me" people who wallow in self-pity in order to win our attention by making us feel sorry for them. As soon as we do, we validate their misery – and they get the energy boost they need to feel better.

The way to deal with these Control Dramas is very simple, and it is the same for all four of them. All you have to do is NAME their Control Drama out loud – in other words, name what they are doing. And you do this by asking them, in a neutral voice (neither afraid nor aggressive) WHY they are doing it:

For the Intimidator:
– *"Why are you trying to intimidate me?"*

For the Interrogator:
– *"Why are you interrogating – or criticising – me?"*

For the Aloof:
– *"Why are you being so aloof?"*

For the Poor Me:
– *"Why are you feeling sorry for yourself?"*

Asking the question "Why?" means they have to answer. They will always deny it, of course, but you have now named their Control Drama – and they KNOW you have – so their game is up.

You see, Control Dramas only ever work as a subterfuge. Once a person's Control Drama is out in the open, they can't keep doing it.

As a sales professional, you will come across all four Control Dramas over and over again in your customers.

In the past, these have been the so-called "difficult" clients that can ruin your day. But not any more.

That is why I have saved this powerful skill for last. It not only prevents you from having to cope with their manipulative tactics… it will save you time and money as well.

Try it. It works like magic!

Last word:
The secret to success

...in life, as well as in sales

MY passionate wish for you as we come to the end of this sales program is that all the skills you have learnt in this little book will transform both your career and your personal life in the same way they have transformed mine.

Before we say goodbye, I just want to take a moment to wish you well on your journey and to remind you that there is actually only one journey worth taking… and that is the journey within.

That is what all my books and all my seminars focus on above everything else.

Everything you are seeking is already inside you.

Right now, as you read this, you possess all the keys to all the imaginary doors that stand between where you are now and where you want your dream life to be… financially, physically, emotionally and spiritually.

So please relax into your life. Be happy now, right now... where you are NOW.

Don't look for a reason to be happy.

Be unreasonably happy!

Remember what I said at the very beginning of this book... it all starts with FEELING GOOD.

If you are happy first, success will follow you wherever you go.

You will achieve all your goals.

You will live a long, prosperous and fulfilled life.

And best of all you will annoy the crap out of everyone else!

* * *

Until we meet again... love your work.

And love your life!

Simon

Also in the "10 Steps" series

Turn your dream life into your REAL life

There is only one thing standing between where you are now and where you want your dream life to be. And it's not that you are too old, or too young, or too poor, or too lazy, or too busy... or any other excuse.

It's fear.

10 Steps to Break Through Fear takes you step by step through 10 simple yet effective techniques to help you break through all of your limiting beliefs about who you THINK you are and what you THINK you are capable of achieving.

When you learn to master your fears and free yourself from the limiting beliefs that are holding you back, everything in your life changes. Your weight drops off, your addictions are gone, your money worries are gone… all of it is gone.

* * *

This small but powerful 122-page book will teach you how to tap into your inner power and take control of your life, starting today.

You can buy "*10 Steps to Break Through Fear*" now as a paperback or eBook from Amazon and other good online booksellers – or you can save by ordering your hard copy paperback directly from the publisher via email at simonhfirth@gmail.com

Other books by Simon

Create LASTING love and passion

Leap into Love is based on Simon's popular relationships workshop of the same name. It takes the form of a four-week course (one chapter for each day, with weekends off!) in which you will learn how to create a close, loving relationship with your partner and all your loved ones.

And if you are single you will learn how to attract your dream partner into your life… and keep them there.

You will also learn why relationships are so important to your personal growth, and you will discover that there are four different types of relationship, but only one that can give you lasting love and happiness.

Above all, you will learn how to create a deep and passionate relationship with the one person in your life who needs and deserves your love the most… YOU.

* * *

Leap into Love is jam-packed with life-changing information and is the amalgamation of everything Simon knows about love, self-love and relationships after a lifetime spent studying why we have them and what makes them work, or not.

It is subtitled "A Course in Creating Miracles" because there are no greater miracles than being able to manifest peace, love and passion – with no fear – every single day for the rest of your life.

* * *

You can buy *"Leap into Love"* as a 350-page paperback or eBook from Amazon and other good online booksellers – or you can save by ordering your hard copy paperback today directly from the publisher via email at simonhfirth@gmail.com

Give your child the gift of happiness

Your child's ability to communicate effectively is the single most important skill they will ever learn, and yet astonishingly it is not taught in school.

How to Raise a Happy Child will first teach you how to become a Master Communicator who is able to reach your child on the deepest level.

Then it will show you how to teach all your new skills to your children so they can grow up to become Master Communicators as well.

This will be the most valuable skill they will ever learn for every area of their life:

– They will be able to express themselves and connect with everyone they meet on a deep level.

– They will excel at school and then later in their chosen career path.

– They will know precisely how to create lasting and loving relationships with their partner and everyone else in their life.

– Above all, they will grow up to become optimistic, confident and HAPPY adults.

* * *

You can buy *"How to Raise a Happy Child"* as a 374-page paperback or eBook from Amazon and other good online booksellers – or you can save by ordering your hard copy paperback directly from the publisher via email at simonhfirth@gmail.com

Lessons from Tyson

The rescue dog who rescued me back

Simon H Firth

(Author of 'Messages from your Self', 'Leap Into Love' and 'How to Raise a Happy Child')

Please help rescue our furry friends!

Simon's most personal book to date tells the remarkable story of his faithful rescue dog Tyson – or "Tysie Bear", as he was known to all his many friends.

In this moving little illustrated pocket book, Simon shares some of the life-changing lessons that Tyson taught him about friendship, unconditional love and the existence of the spirit world.

Tyson has sadly gone to that world, but his lessons about life and love will stay with you forever. And his unique gifts will resonate in your heart long after you have closed the covers on this unforgettable book.

This charity book is a must for all animal lovers, and especially those who have loved and lost a furry soulmate.

* * *

How you can help...

Please buy as many copies of the book as you can because every single cent you spend goes to charity.

All the money Simon Firth Seminars makes from the sale of this book goes to animal shelters and rescue organisations around the world to help find much-needed loving families for homeless, rejected and unwanted pets.

Of course, if you can donate to your local animal rescue shelter as well, please do. Hundreds of thousands of homeless pets are destroyed around the world every year... so every dollar counts.

You can buy "Lessons from Tyson" as an 84-page illustrated paperback or eBook from Amazon and other good online booksellers – or you can save by ordering your hard copy paperback directly from the publisher via email at simonhfirth@gmail.com

On behalf of Tyson... THANK YOU!

BRAND NEW!

A guide book for finding your bliss

In his ground-breaking new book *Messages from your Self*, Simon takes you on a remarkable journey of discovery inside the secret code of the universe, where he shows you how to use the ancient art of numerology to guide you to a life of unending bliss.

You will be astonished at how something as simple as your date of birth can reveal so much about who you are, why you are here and how you can live the life of your dreams.

There is nothing new about numerology. It has been used by every major civilisation throughout history. But no one has ever been able to explain WHY it works.

Until now.

The reason will amaze you because it not only explains how the universe is structured, it also reveals how it was created, by what... and why.

* * *

"Messages from your Self" is confronting, controversial and right at the cutting edge of modern spiritual awareness.

At 828 pages long, it has taken Simon 21 years to research and write and it is available now as a paperback and an eBook from Amazon and other good online booksellers.

You can also order the paperback version from the publisher via email at simonhfirth@gmail.com

ço